CHILDREN
OF
WELFARE

JOAN J. JOHNSON

TWENTY-FIRST CENTURY BOOKS

A Division of Henry Holt and Company • New York

Twenty-First Century Books
A Division of Henry Holt and Company, Inc.
115 West 18th Street
New York, NY 10011

Henry Holt® and colophon are trademarks of
Henry Holt and Company, Inc.
Publishers since 1866

Library of Congress Cataloging-in-Publication Data
Johnson, Joan (Joan J.)
Children of welfare / Joan J. Johnson.
p.   cm.
Includes bibliographical references and index.
Summary: Describes what it means to grow up with parents
on welfare, the history of the welfare system, and its future.
1. Aid to families with dependent children programs—
United States—Juvenile literature. 2. Welfare recipients—United
States—Juvenile literature. 3. Public welfare—United States—
Juvenile literature. [1. Public welfare.] I. Title.
HV699.J65 1997
362.71'3'0973—dc21   96-45193
                                                                                          CIP
                                                                                          AC

ISBN 0-8050-2985-0
First Edition—1997

DESIGNED BY KELLY SOONG

Printed in the United States of America
All first editions are printed on acid-free paper ∞.

1 3 5 7 9 10 8 6 4 2

CONTENTS

One   The Faces of Poverty   5

Two   "The Welfare"   15

Three   No One to Turn To   31

Four   Family Ties   43

Five   Home Sweet Home   59

Six   Failure to Thrive   69

Seven   Unequal Education   76

Eight   The Streets   87

Nine   Welfare's Successes and Failures   95

Ten   Of Frogs and Futures   105

Source Notes   113

Further Reading   122

Index   126

ONE

THE FACES OF POVERTY

Gina Clemans wants to go to college after she finishes high school, but she also knows that wanting does not mean getting. For Gina, college is likely to remain a dream. She says that when she tries to visualize her future, "I just see a blank. . . . Nothing but a blank." Gina grew up in the Seattle, Washington, public-housing development built for low-income families. Roxbury Village is surrounded by fences. Inside, the sounds, the food smells, the languages, the cultures, the colors of its residents intermingle. When she was a child, Gina didn't notice the poverty. She was too young to care much about trash cans filled to overflowing or broken glass, too inexperienced to see anything special in boarded windows. "I didn't know any better," said Gina. "I was only a child."[1] Now Gina believes that the fences surrounding Roxbury Village were meant "to keep us penned," making it impossible to break out of a life of hard work, of living day by day on the edge of catastrophe, and of having hopes and dreams dashed.

In Fort Lauderdale, Florida, little Autumn ———— was lucky to be a healthy baby. Her parents, Tina and Steve, both only eighteen years old, were too poor to get prenatal counseling. When Autumn was about to be born, Tina walked into the Broward General Medical Center and said, "I'm here. Help me."[2] But while Autumn was lucky to have no birth defects, she was not so lucky when the time came to go home. She has spent her early life in a 104-bed shelter for homeless teenagers because her parents cannot afford a place of their own. "I didn't expect to become a parent as soon as we did," her mother admits. "After it happens [getting pregnant], you think about birth control. But we didn't once think about abortion or adoption."[3]

TURNING TO WELFARE

When disaster strikes, when someone is laid off, when someone gets sick, when a housing complex is torn down, emptying the poor out onto the streets, welfare is the only alternative. For some, life on welfare will be temporary. As we shall see in the next chapter, that is the case for most welfare recipients. Welfare will be the low point from which most will struggle upward. They will use their time on welfare to gain the skills they need to increase career opportunities. For others, welfare will become a way of life. Some will be born to it and know no other way. For all, however, welfare will be a hard time and a hard place.

THE INFANTS

For some, hard times begin at birth. At Broward General Medical Center in Florida, a fragile thirteen-day-old baby weighing under two pounds is reminded to breathe by the incubator in which he sleeps. Born prematurely to a cocaine-addicted mother, the child will probably be blind. Right now, he suffers from seizures. His arms and legs shake and convulse repeatedly. He is his mother's fourth child, the only one who has lived. But he belongs to the welfare system. "Nobody wants him," the doctor says.[4] He will spend most of the first year of his life in this hospital ward. After that, his future is unclear.

Across the room, another boy, now three weeks old and only four pounds, waits to be taken home by his fifteen-year-old mother. She also has a ten-month-old baby. "He's going to be another toy for her to play with. It's pointless to try to teach her about parenting," a nurse says, shaking her head. "She's not going to do it when she gets home."[5]

In Washington, D.C., the cribs of infants T, M, and D stand in a line at the back of a small, dreary ward on the second floor of Columbia General. No one comes to visit them. They are healthy, thriving babies who should have gone home long ago. When their mothers left the hospital, they gave authorities fake addresses and telephone numbers. They were addicts so anxious to get back to the streets that they didn't have time to name their children.

"Boarder babies," as these children are called, will learn to walk in the hospital. Their only human contact comes from the nurses and doctors who are helpless to do anything about their plight. Each year, the more than twenty-two thousand children deserted by their parents must wait in hospitals to be placed in foster care. Three-quarters test positive for drugs at birth. Many are HIV positive.[6]

THE CHILDREN

While some become children of welfare at birth, others will experience home and family problems that force them into the welfare system during childhood. Sean Mitaynes was one such child. "I don't know where my father's at. From the age of five till about nine or ten, I didn't live with my mother. I lived in different foster homes and stuff."[7] According to Sean, many of those homes weren't much better than living with his drug-addicted mother. In one home he was beaten; in another, he was often locked in a closet for long periods. He became a problem at school and stayed back more than once. When his mother finally got custody of Sean, they had a chance to be together only a short time before she died. "Just so you know, my mom died of cancer . . . she had cancer of the uterus," Sean maintains. But then he adds, "She was already dying from AIDS from shooting drugs and stuff, and doing other things, whatever."[8]

Sean's view of the world is old and wizened for someone just eighteen years of age. He has seen it all. To survive, he has learned to mistrust everyone and everything they say. His inability to trust almost cost him his life. While staying with his last foster family, he tried to hang himself. He had already turned blue before others discovered his limp body and cut him down. "I did something really stupid. I tried to . . . how can I explain it? I didn't try to kill myself, exactly . . . I just wanted to be independent."[9]

Christopher Muskus lives with his mother, Linda, and his nine-year-old sister, Jessica, just a few blocks away from the state capitol building in Hartford, Connecticut. For a share of their drugs, Chris's mother is very good at finding veins in the legs and arms of addicts whose circulatory system has been ruined by years of "shooting up." Linda's back room is streaked with their blood. The children are not allowed in the room when adults are shooting up. "They try to hide everything," Christopher says. Still Christopher knows that he can watch what is going on through a crack in the kitchen wall.[10] Sometimes more than a dozen junkies use Linda's back room while the children wait and watch television. Above the children hangs Jessica's painting of a basket of fruit. It won a Hartford art contest.

Christopher and Jessica stay out of the house as much as possible. Their mother gives them candy money to go. Their lives are a turmoil. When they are not in school, they have friends, neighborhood boys and girls with whom they spend hours hunting for stray cats, teasing junkies in the alleys, or just watching life on the streets. Baby, their German shepherd, is always with them, even waiting outside McDonald's while they look for leftovers. One of Jessica's favorite tricks is putting sugar packets into McDonald's coffee creamers and drinking them like shots. Since the children are on their own for dinner, they also rummage through the trash for edibles. They come home long after dark. At bedtime, even if no addicts are using the room, Chris prefers to sleep on the floor in a closet, where it's safe.

In the winter of 1993, Chicago police seeking a drug peddler knocked on the door of a city apartment just before midnight. They discovered nineteen welfare children living in one small, filthy apartment. According to reporters Michele Ingrassia and John McCormick:

> each discovery [yielded] a new, more stunning find. In the dining room, police said, a half-dozen children lay asleep on a bed, their tiny bodies intertwined like kittens. On the floor beside them, two toddlers tussled with a mutt over a bone they had grabbed from the dog's dish. In the living room, four others huddled on a hardwood floor, crowded beneath a single blanket . . . [They found] . . . the last of the 19 asleep under a mound of dirty clothes; one 4-year-old, gnarled by cerebral palsy, bore welts and bruises.[11]

The plaster was crumbling, and roaches scurried around clumps of rat droppings. Crusty dishes filled the sink. The refrigerator was empty. None of the six mothers who lived in this filthy apartment were at home at the time. Yet between them, they were collecting $4,500 a month in Aid to Families with Dependent Children (AFDC) and food stamps intended for the support of their children.

Parental neglect, incompetence, and drug and alcohol abuse place many young people in jeopardy; others end up on welfare because of teenage pregnancy. Sixteen-year-old Erica George lives in Madison, Arkansas. She is a ninth grader at Forrest City High School, a half-hour bus ride away from home. Erica is also the mother of an eighteen-month-old boy. Both of them live with Erica's mother on a dirt road called Dogwood Acres. Erica's mother has nine children by four different fathers. She has lived most of her life on welfare. Probably Erica will too. Her boyfriend and the father of her son, Eric Mills, "ain't able to help her out right now. I'm trying my best," he says. "Trying to get a job at the City Hall as a maintenance worker, but you know how it is."[12] Eric dropped out of school. Unable to find work, he hangs out in the local park, playing basketball.

While babies having babies is nothing new, the number of children choosing to get pregnant *is* new. Many girls admit that they knew exactly what they were doing when they got pregnant. Leslie Morris, a Los Angeles social worker who specializes in teenage mothers, says:

> When the girls talk about their feelings with me, the one thing that always comes through is a need to have something to hold on to, that belongs to them, that no one can take away. There's a feeling of deprivation and hopelessness in their lives. You can hear it in the conversations they have today. "Give me a reason not to have a child at this stage of my life, when my future looks dim, and all around me people are dying and getting shot. Why not have a child?"[13]

Many of them know their boyfriends will be unreliable fathers. Raychelle, a member of Morris's group, explains:

"My children have two different fathers. Both of them were [drug] dealers. I don't know what they're doing now. I have a new boyfriend."[14] Kim, another group member, says, "I just broke up with my daughter's father. He's a drug dealer." Janine, a third member, says she hasn't seen her child's father in months.

In Carmichael, California, Cindy K., age seventeen, is already the mother of two sons. Each has a different father, although Cindy never married either one of them. They live in a one-bedroom apartment that contains, in total, an old couch, a table, and a bed. Cindy had the first baby "on purpose, for someone to love me."[15] She didn't feel the same way about the second baby, whom she planned to put up for adoption. But her boyfriend, at age twenty-seven already the father of six other children by three other women, refused to let her. If it hadn't been for welfare, Cindy admits, she could never have kept the children. She would have given them both up for adoption. Now, despite the fact that she feels ill-prepared to be a mother, she believes it is up to her to make sure her children "have a better life than I did."

Cindy is an example of the teenage pregnancy welfare cycle. She was born an illegitimate child and reared on welfare. Her mother was a substance abuser who admits to teaching Cindy "to roll joints when she was six years old." By age fourteen, Cindy took up with some rather tough friends, began taking drugs, and dropped out of school. She continued to live with her mother through the births of both of her children, but because they often fought, Cindy arranged for welfare to pay the rent on an apartment of her own. Welfare gives her $607 a month through Aid to Families with Dependent Children, $216 in food stamps, and Medicaid for health costs. Meanwhile, the boys' fathers come to visit their sons. Cindy still has feelings for them both but voices anger that "I wasn't alone when these kids were made, but [now] I'm here to do everything by myself."[16]

Alex and Cyrus, her sons, go with her to a high school for teenage mothers and stay in the school's day care center while Cindy attends classes. At night, she takes care of their needs, then does her homework. Cindy believes she is going to be all right, that she can make it through the hardships. She doesn't want to remain on welfare and hopes to get married someday. Meanwhile, she wants to become a secretary. That means entering trade school in the fall. Unfortunately, she has no one to care for her boys while she goes to school. Cindy says she has "not thought that far ahead yet."[17]

SINGLE PARENTHOOD

The combination of pregnancy, dropping out of school, and single parenthood is often a formula for disaster. There are no jobs for these young parents—at least, no jobs that can pay them the wages needed to support a family. Most of the jobs that they qualify for are unskilled labor jobs, often without the benefits of vacation or sick days, often paying just the minimum wage. They are primarily temporary jobs, the kinds that teenagers take in the summer or that other people accept while they're preparing for some other career. They are the kind transient people take as they come and go from one place to another. Or they are seasonal jobs, meaning that no sooner will a young person begin bringing home a paycheck than he or she will be let go. There are, of course, migratory jobs—following the crops—and there are other jobs that almost no one would choose to do. That is why they are available. Very few jobs that are open to unskilled laborers offer training and advancement.

Then, of course, once the child is born, there is the constant problem of child care. Decent child care is hard to find, and it is expensive. Even if a parent has managed to find a job and a sitter, infants are often sick and must be kept home. While a professional with a good employment record and excellent company benefits can miss work to care for a sick child, young people with no job histories and with no benefits will more likely be let go. Their employers have made little investment in them and hundreds of other unemployed hopefuls are waiting to fill their positions.

STAYING ON WELFARE

To survive, a single parent must soon learn to forget dreams and to face reality. As time passes, youthful idealism usually gives way to cynicism. Denise B., who is now twenty-nine, lives in the Harold Ickes Homes, funded by the Chicago, Illinois, Housing Authority. It's called a "lock-down building" because crime is so rife there that armed guards had to be hired to patrol the premises. In many ways, Denise had everything going for her. She attended a respected parochial school in Chicago, maintained a B average, and lived in a home her parents actually owned. Both of Denise's parents had good jobs that paid well enough for her and her three sisters to attend private school.

But Denise fell in love with Joe and then became pregnant at age fifteen. When she recalls her plans to become a lawyer, she says: "It just slips away if you don't stay with it. It slips away."[18] While Denise maintains that she'd like to work, she explains that she'd have to earn a lot to beat welfare. She has thought all that through. "You've got to look at the medical, the food and everything else." Getting a good job would mean going back to school and working her way up. "That's going to take time," she says. "It's a lot of work, and I ain't guaranteed to get nothing." Welfare, on the other hand, is guaranteed. In Denise's mind, staying on welfare is better than having dreams, than going to school, than working her way up some corporate ladder. Welfare, she says, "is an enabler. It's not that you want to be in that situation. But it's there. We always know."[19]

While for some, welfare has been a way up and out of poverty, too many young people find themselves trapped and without hope. Journalist Michael Leahy describes seventeen-year-old Tangela Livingston, already the mother of three boys. Tangela, he writes:

> dreams of nothing, the weight of her miseries literally bending her over in the Lee County Clinic, her body slumped while she mumbles into the seat of her chair, complaining that the child support payments of her children's father do not bring her enough; that she doesn't know enough about anything to get a good job; that she can't get married to her children's father because the government would cut her welfare; that she won't go back to school because she doesn't like the people or the place. Tangela laughs when asked what she sees herself doing in the future, a stooped child utterly devoid of a vision of herself, a dropout bereft of skills or prospects.[20]

Or there is Adie, who admits that "doing acid every day doesn't help you very much." She too seems to have lost hope. "The world sucks. It's always like that—anytime there's somebody you respect, they always f—— up or die."[21]

As we shall see in the next chapter, the welfare system is a costly bureaucracy that has failed to keep its promises. While welfare has provided food and shelter, its past policies have failed to prevent, and in some cases have even encouraged, welfare dependency. While the sweeping welfare reforms that were signed into law in August 1996 are aimed at correcting the problem, it will be years, if not decades, before real improvements, if any, occur.

"THE WELFARE"

Welfare has been around just long enough that many U.S. citizens think it has always existed. For most people under the age of sixty, reading about, hearing about, and often complaining about welfare is something that they've experienced their entire lives. So it is easy to jump to the conclusion that welfare is something everyone is *entitled* to if he or she needs it and that it *will always* remain.

Nothing could be farther from the truth. While charitable individuals and charitable groups have always helped the poor, a federally instituted and administered system is actually quite new. If any of the young people we met in the last chapter had been born a century or two earlier, even a few decades earlier, their fates might have been far different.

Public-subsidized housing for Gina Clemans and her family didn't exist until this century. Young, single mothers who have children out-of-wedlock are indeed no new story. But in earlier times they were publicly shamed and isolated. Their futures were bleak. For a single woman to have a child out-of-wedlock was in many ways worse than death, because women had none of the job opportunities they do today, and their assumed lack of morality made them pariahs in their own towns. Many were forced into a life of prostitution just to feed themselves; most could not continue to care for their children, who had to be given over to orphanages.

WELFARE IN INDUSTRIAL TIMES

During the 1800s, the United States changed from a farming society to an industrial society. Jobs were to be had in the cities where factories were springing up in great throbbing clusters. Masses of people flooded to them looking for work. What soon became known as the working class emerged in these cities. Through their unions, working people fought long and hard to gain a better life for themselves and their families. Because of their efforts, state governments eventually provided for their widows if they had been left with young children. The Mothers' Assistance program was among the first public welfare programs. This program stipulated, however, that those in need had to verify their fitness for aid by proving their moral character. As few as one out of every ten deserving widows actually got help.

ORPHANAGES

In New York City, Charles Brace was astounded and sickened by the "little girls who flitted about with baskets and wrapped in old shawls [who] became familiar with vice before they were out of childhood."[1] Brace believed that at least part of the problem was that taxes were too high, forcing up rents beyond the reach of poor people. But he also believed that taxes were just part of the problem. First, he tried giving directly to those youngsters most in need. What dismayed him was that "if you put a comfortable coat on the first idle and ragged lad who applies, the next day fifty who are not in need will show up to get jackets for nothing." He realized that unless changes "touch habits of life and the inner forces which form character," their effect would be "superficial and comparatively useless."[2] And while shelters might be fine for adults, Brace claimed that "the child, most of all, needs individual care and sympathy."[3]

So Brace set up several lodging houses for abandoned children, where boys and girls received a bed, classes in reading and industrial arts, and Bible lessons. These lodging houses, however, were only meant to be transitional safe places. Brace wanted to get children off the streets and turn them into respectable adults. To do so, he believed it best to place his "orphans" in adoptive homes in the countryside. There they could receive discipline, love, and a sense of values from their new parents. By the late 1870s Brace's New York Children's Aid Society was sending approximately four thousand children a year out of the city on "orphan trains" that dropped them off in towns across the nation.

Unquestionably, this program had dangers. Farm families might be less motivated by kindness than by the need for cheap labor. These young children could have been easily abused. In the long run, however, Brace believed the rewards were worth the risks. Brace's orphan trains made a huge difference in the lives of thousands of children who had no prospects and no hope before being adopted. One young graduate of Brace's program wrote: "To be taken from the gutters of New York City and placed in a college is almost a miracle."[4] Brace's orphans became bankers, businessmen, merchants, and farmers. Three of them became governors.

WELFARE DURING THE DEPRESSION

It was the crisis created by the Depression in the 1930s that set the stage for welfare as we know it today. Conditions everywhere in the United States were so bad that people lined up for blocks to get a meager handout of food. Hobo camps swarming with hundreds of homeless people sprang up beside railroad lines and highways as the hungry traveled from one place to another looking for work. Mammoth demonstrations demanding government aid led to growing tension and police reprisals. Many demonstrators were killed. The situation became so explosive that President Franklin D. Roosevelt, fearing a revolution, put together a group of programs that he and his advisors called the New Deal. New Deal programs built libraries, hospitals, schools, roads, and parks. Agencies provided work for everyone from artists to carpenters. Older citizens began getting Social Security payments once they retired. Those with jobs got unemployment insurance. From then on, people who were temporarily out of work received cash payments to carry them for a time.

Roosevelt never intended that anyone should receive welfare permanently. These programs were to be transitional until the recipient found permanent work. He said, "Continued dependence upon relief induces a spiritual and moral disintegration fundamentally destructive to the nation's fiber. To dole out relief in this way is to administer a narcotic, a subtle destroyer of the human spirit."[5]

JOHNSON'S WAR ON POVERTY

After the Depression, this country saw three decades of expansion and economic good health. Many Americans made a great deal of money, and others, with the right skills and the right education, moved up in the world. They owned houses and cars. They joined country clubs and took vacations. They sent their children to college so that their sons and daughters could have even greater prospects. They became the middle class.

But not everyone moved up. Some were left behind to live in poverty in cities and in depressed rural areas such as Appalachia. By the 1960s their plight had become so worrisome that President Lyndon B. Johnson declared a war on poverty. Congress instituted several measures to help the poor help themselves out of poverty through job training programs. Food stamps provided nutritional aid to the poor, and government-subsidized medical insurance assisted those who could not pay for medical treatment. Finally, under Johnson, the widowed mothers' assistance program became Aid to Families With Dependent Children (AFDC).

Johnson's "war on poverty" increased the number of those receiving government aid to four million by the end of the 1960s. People were getting aid who had previously been denied it, and additional numbers needed help when unemployment figures rose.

As in Colonial times, once the numbers on welfare grew and the tax burden became too great, critics of welfare raised serious questions about these programs. AFDC had expanded to such a size that the old widowed mothers' program was unrecognizable. Recipients were characterized as "primarily inner-city black women who . . . 'mindlessly accumulated children.'"[6] By the time President Ronald Reagan dubbed them "welfare queens who drove Cadillacs and used Food Stamps to buy liquor" in the 1980s, the nation's patience was wearing thin.

THE IMMIGRATION PROBLEM

Immigrants, too, have taken a share of the blame. Not since the turn of the century has immigration policy caused such controversy. The nation's economic ability to absorb the swelling rolls of refugees and legal and illegal immigrants and to provide them with welfare and unemployment benefits is a matter of grave concern to many, especially in those six or seven states where these immigrants have tended to cluster. "I understand, in the past, 'Give me your tired, your poor.' Today, the U.S. has to look at our own huddled masses first," former Colorado governor Richard Lamm told *Business Week* magazine.[7]

These fears have created a backlash. In California, backlash took the form of legislation that would deny all but emergency services to illegal immigrants, including education and welfare, and would require teachers, law-enforcement officers, and health-care workers to report anyone suspected of being an illegal alien to immigration authorities. Governor Pete Wilson also filed lawsuits against the federal government for the $3 billion a year that 1.5 million illegal aliens cost his state. Proposition 187 was supported by California voters in a landslide decision, but its legality is being questioned in the federal courts.

Some believe that illegal immigrants should not have the same rights as those here legally, that such support puts unfair burdens on the few states where illegals tend to congregate, and that their countries of origin should be responsible for their education and health care. Others worry that not providing health care and education could backfire on the whole nation, causing far more serious problems in the future, such as tuberculosis outbreaks. Until the courts make a decision, the proposition cannot be implemented.

WHAT IS WELFARE?

As we shall see later, many camps have developed around the issue of welfare, with some groups fighting to maintain welfare as it is, others fighting to reform it, and still others proposing to get rid of it altogether. But to understand their arguments, it is important to know exactly what welfare programs exist and which programs seem to have the most problems.

Welfare is not just one program; it is many. Each of the programs that make up "welfare" is designed to aid a specific aspect of the recipient's daily life. All are designed to help the poor and/or needy survive. Some of the programs are short term. Unemployment insurance, for example, provides the head of a family with funds to replace at least some of the income he or she lost when let go from a job. It is temporary in that one can receive unemployment benefits for twenty-six weeks and must be actively looking for another job during that time. Usually, once the twenty-six weeks are up, a still-unemployed person has to apply for welfare. On occasion, unemployment benefits may be extended.

Long-term aid is a very different kind of aid. Until 1996, when President Clinton signed the welfare reform bill, long-term aid such as AFDC and Medicaid had no time limits attached to them. Long-term aid was designed to help those in poverty climb out of it and to support them in the process. Medicaid, for example, insures that the poor get medical treatment; it pays their doctor and hospital bills. Free school lunch programs insure that needy children get at least one wholesome, nutritious meal five days a week. Food stamps are another insurance against hunger. Food stamps are issued to needy families, and they, in turn, use the stamps as a form of "money" to buy necessary groceries. The stamps can only be used for foodstuffs. Twenty-seven million Americans received food stamps in 1993.

To receive any form of welfare, a family's eligibility must be "means-tested." A government official checks the applicant's situation to determine that the family's income is below a certain level. If it is, then the family can begin to receive cash payments and other forms of assistance. While some families are granted participation in a few welfare programs, others receive literally every kind of welfare available.

AFDC

While Medicaid is the most costly welfare program, it is not the one that has caused the greatest furor among taxpayers. That singular honor goes to Aid to Families with Dependent Children. AFDC was intended to keep families intact. Anyone who had a child, legitimate or not, widowed, married, single or not, was eligible for the program, provided that a parent was "continuously absent from home, incapacitated, dead or unemployed." In 1994, four million families, fifteen million people, received AFDC.[8] Most of these families were headed by single mothers.

All AFDC families received monthly checks that differed based on need, the number of children in the family, and the cost of living in each state. The federal government paid more than half the cost; the state in which the recipient lived paid the rest. Each state determined who would be eligible and how much each family would receive. The monthly check for a family of three could be as little as $120 in Mississippi, where rents and grocery costs are low, or as much as $924 in Alaska, where necessities are more costly.

When President Clinton signed into legislation HR3734 on August 1, 1996, the sixty-one-year-old guarantee of federal welfare checks to all eligible mothers and children, AFDC, was replaced by a new program, Temporary Assistance for Needy Families. Under TANF, states will receive "block grants" of money formerly used for AFDC by the federal government. They will have "wide discretion" on how that money will be used, but the sums allotted to states will increase or decrease based on how successful the states are at moving people off welfare and into jobs and at reducing out-of-wedlock births. TANF will place severe new restrictions on former AFDC families, including required work hours and cumulative time limits. No one knows what the full effect of HR3734 will be, especially regarding dependent children now protected by the government.

Many critics of welfare believe that instead of a life-ladder out of poverty, AFDC encouraged people *not* to work and fostered dependence rather than independence. Those who work and pay taxes resent those who don't work, who instead continue to live on the public dole. Working taxpayers are frustrated that they must struggle to pay their bills and support welfare recipients as well. "I see people buying food with food stamps, and they're buying better stuff than I am," one Chicago, Illinois, woman complained.[9]

Most welfare recipients need welfare for a matter of only a few months or years. They use that time to pull themselves and their lives together, to plan, and to acquire some job skills. It is hoped they will be unaffected by HR3734's time restrictions. Under the new law, adults receiving welfare benefits are required to begin working within two years of receiving aid. Single parents will have to work twenty hours a week in 1996, but that time requirement will increase to thirty hours by the year 2000. Two-parent families will have to work thirty-five hours a week.

The new bill also sets time limits on the number of years block grant money can be given to recipients. Adults who have received welfare for more than five years are prohibited from receiving federal block grant money, although states and local governments can use their own funds as they chose. This part of the bill is aimed at chronic welfare dependency. While the great majority of recipients received AFDC for less than a total of two years, between 1.5 and 2 million households have remained on welfare more than eight years. They lack education. They lack employment skills. They are the poorest of all of the underclass. They are of all races, although a disproportionate number of them are inner-city black single mothers.[10] No one seems to know what should be done about these seemingly hopeless families that have languished on welfare decade after decade, generation after generation. When their benefits are cut, where will they go? How will they eat? And most important, what will happen to their children?

THE NEED FOR WELFARE REFORM

While almost everyone agrees that something has to be done about these "permanent" welfare families and about the policies that seem to foster them, no one has been able to come up with a fail-safe way to correct the problem. Some people think that welfare reform must offer mothers all-inclusive and extremely expensive training and schooling. To participate in such programs, recipients also need day care for their children. Once they are actually working, parents must also be granted Medicaid until they are on their feet, perhaps for a year or longer. To be sure that recipients take their job responsibilities seriously, someone must also take a look at the reasons they were absent or late, verify them, and if the excuses are flimsy, find ways to "punish" or sanction parents so that it doesn't happen again.

Other critics say that putting people to work isn't the real problem. The real problem is reducing the number of illegitimate children being born in mushrooming numbers in every state in the country. According to these reformers, welfare encourages out-of-wedlock children by paying mothers more each month for every child they have. "Out-of-wedlock births is the single most important social problem of our time," Charles Murray, a scholar and welfare critic, wrote in the early 1990s.[11] It is this trend that has produced the growing "underclass" in the black community.

According to Murray, that same trend will soon be affecting whites. In Sioux City, Idaho, for example, a midwestern town with typically midwestern values, one of every three children born each day is illegitimate. Worse, one of every seven is being born to a teenage mother who chose to get pregnant.[12] According to Murray:

> the nation's low-income communities, both black and white, are increasingly peopled by the grown-up children of unmarried young women and men who were utterly unequipped to be parents. As we have moved into the second, third, and fourth generations of unmarried parenthood, the rest of the networks that once stepped in have also disappeared, for without marriage in one generation, aunts and uncles and grandparents become scarce in the next. As families have broken down, so have the neighborhood institutions for which families are the building blocks.[13]

Murray believes that removing the safety net that welfare has created for those who find themselves in need of assistance, or at least removing a part of the net, would discourage out-of-wedlock pregnancies. Women would be not only less likely to get pregnant, but also emphatically discouraged from doing so by their mothers, fathers, sisters, brothers, and grandparents who might be obliged to take up the slack left by government reductions in aid. In apparent response to this theory, the welfare overhaul legislation just signed by President Clinton gives states the option to deny welfare to unwed parents under the age of eighteen unless they live with an adult (parent) and attend school.

William Bennett, another critic of present-day welfare, writes that "There can be little doubt that the message our laws have been sending our young people and their parents has been the profoundly demoralizing one that we expect little, and hold ourselves answerable for still less."[14] The old notion that people must work to get ahead has been replaced by a new view that it is the system that is to blame for poverty. Those "hurt" by the system should be "entitled" to certain benefits. The only way to get those benefits is to appear to be incapable of dealing with problems. Consequently, people are *encouraged* to behave in self-defeating ways. "Knowing they can get into the Job Corps training program, more kids drop out of school. Knowing they can get welfare benefits, more young single women have babies out of wedlock. The more dysfunctional the behavior, the more the government spends," Murray maintains.[15]

Murray's theory implies that most welfare recipients plan their problems. But according to Peggy Bald, a director of the women's center at Florida Community College in Jacksonville, "You're not dealing with a group that has the energy to plan. They are planning their next meal. You live day to day to day." For example, says Bald, "They are not planning their next child. They'll get pregnant without thinking about it."[16] Whether or not additional children are planned, the new reform bill also gives states the option of denying welfare assistance to children born to welfare recipients, making it very clear that parents who allow more children to be brought into the world will have to spread their benefits thinner to support them.

THE REFORM EFFORTS

It will be months, if not years, before the full effects of HR3734 are felt and the data gathered to evaluate its success or failure. But new welfare reforms cannot be expected to solve all the problems connected to welfare. For one, because different states set their own eligibility standards and benefit levels, the benefits welfare recipients receive vary dramatically from state to state. Additionally, the cost of living in some states is higher than in others.

The consequence is that the states that offer the most positive, effective, and costly programs find they become "welfare magnets" for the needy from other states. On the one hand, it is in the taxpayers' best interests to develop programs that really do lift people out of poverty. Although very costly in the short term, in the long term this approach could possibly end the need for welfare. While taxpayers spend a great deal now, they save far more later. But the approach doesn't work if the masses of those helped off welfare through costly programs are quickly replaced by others crossing state borders to get help their own states do not offer. Even though an optional provision of the new welfare reform act allows states temporarily to limit newcomers' aid to the amount they would have received in their former states, many still worry that their programs are attracting others' welfare problems.

The result is that some new policies are designed to motivate chronic welfare recipients to get off the dole or to force them out of the state. New Jersey no longer provides the extra sixty-four dollars per month per child to welfare mothers who have additional children. Former Governor James Florio, defending the cut, said that "middle-class families can't demand a pay increase because a new baby is coming. Our new law allows welfare recipients to live under those same values."[17]

Wisconsin has decided to cut benefits to families by $100 if a teenage son or daughter who has already had ten unexcused absences from school misses two days of school in a month. In Ohio, teenage mothers who stay in school are rewarded with increased benefits, but those who drop out are punished by decreases.

Massachusetts has cut its rolls 38 percent by making eligibility rules more stringent. Ohio has cut its general assistance benefit to $100 per month and limited participation on welfare to six months per year, which should cut welfare rolls by ninety thousand people. Every state in every part of this country is considering dramatic reforms to cut welfare spending, and when the block grant money created by HR3734 becomes available, certainly other deterrents will be put into place.

THE RECIPIENTS' ATTITUDES

The public's attitude toward the impoverished may have soured over the last several decades, but welfare has not always been all bad. A former editor of the *New York Times Book Review* and a 1960s childhood recipient of welfare, Rosemary Bray, writes: "What fueled our dreams and fired our belief that our lives could change for the better was the promise of the civil rights movement and the war on poverty. Had I been born a few years earlier, or a decade later, I might now be living on welfare in the Robert Taylor Homes or working as a hospital nurse's aid for $6.67 an hour." But Bray was fortunate to need welfare at a time when welfare policies were the most supportive.

Bray worries about the crippling effects welfare has today on its recipients. One New York City Human Resources administrator posed as a welfare applicant to find out exactly what those effects might be. So depersonalizing was the experience that she says: "I ceased to be."[18] Even when she begged for full-time work, she got none.

THE RESENTMENTS

What is it like to grow up on welfare? Kim ——— from New York City describes it: "When I was little, I couldn't understand why our whole lives depended on that green check coming in once a month. I used to hate it. My mother has been on welfare for 20 years."[19] Maxine, also from New York

City, says: "My mother wasn't always on welfare. She used to work for the post office and at a hospital. When she got pregnant, she got on welfare because she couldn't take care of all of us on such little money. I hated it."[20] Kim Williams, from New Jersey, says: "I hate the whole system. They look down on us like we're just dirt on the bottom of their shoes."[21]

While almost everyone on it hates welfare, many of those caught in the welfare cycle see no way out. Raychelle admits: "I don't know when I'll get off welfare. When I graduate from high school, I want to go to college and major in business administration, but I don't know if that will ever happen." And Kim reminds them: "Getting a job didn't help me at all. When I did get a job, they would lower the amount of my welfare check. It was like they were punishing me for working."[22]

One welfare recipient raged at the way she was treated:

> I hate the whole system. . . . I get tired of having to stand on lines that wrap around the corner of the welfare office. I'm also tired of getting humiliated by the welfare workers. They act like they're giving us money from their own pockets. My social worker called me ignorant and a bunch of other names. They look down on people on welfare like we're just dirt on the bottom of their shoes. They just look at me as case number 129623. They don't see me as a human being.[23]

Another added:

> They classify us as young and stupid, and just having babies to get welfare money. The caseworkers just ride on their high horses. They don't know how fast something could bring them down and they could be just like us.[24]

Yet what keeps them going, they all say, is wanting a better life for their children. Their list of desires is short and reasonable: a clean, safe home, a job, and getting off welfare. "Just lying around being on the state, that's not the way I want to do it and that's not what I want for my children," says Kathy Stevens of Norwalk, Connecticut. Kathy left high school one-third of a credit short of what she needed for a diploma. "It was a mistake," she admits. She has been on welfare for six years. In that time, she had five children. "We fail, but we don't have to be failures."[25]

THREE

NO ONE TO
TURN TO

By juggling data about the average cost of things such as shelter, food, and clothing, we can determine how much money a family needs in order to pay for these necessities. If we then listed the incomes of every household highest to lowest and drew a line under the last family income on the list that exceeded the "necessary income" amount, we would have located the "poverty line." Any family income below that line is considered "impoverished."

In one of the richest countries in the world, one would think that very few families live below the poverty line. Yet nothing is farther from the truth. Approximately one of every three African Americans, nearly that same ratio of Hispanics, and more than one in every ten white Americans don't have enough money to pay for even their most basic needs. All told, today nearly one of every four children age eighteen or younger lives below the poverty line. That rate is higher than any other industrialized nation in the world.[1] The numbers of adults and children are mind boggling: 24.5 million whites, 10.6 million African Americans, and 6.6 million Hispanics live in poverty. In all, 41.7 million Americans![2]

It would be bad enough if these numbers remained somewhat constant, but they have not, and most likely they will not in the future. If projections are correct, they will continue to rise. If poverty is cyclical, which most experts agree it is, then welfare children who go on to have children of their own may increase the poverty ratio to one-third or even one-half of all children. Consider the ramifications! While poverty might not inescapably lead to other social problems, poor children are certainly at higher risk of having serious health and education problems. And those problems, multiplied by millions of young people, are certain to impact the rest of society.

RURAL POVERTY

Poverty exists everywhere. B.J. is ten years old. He and his dad live in a ramshackle shantytown just outside of Hazard, Kentucky. They keep warm on cold nights with a potbellied coal stove. Their shack has electricity, but no sink or toilet. The house is grimy. Dirty dishes and half-eaten food are scattered about on window sills and tables. B.J. uses his pellet gun to shoot at rats.

B.J.'s father never got through high school. He used to drive a school bus, but now, after two heart attacks, the most he does is knock plastic fittings from discarded aluminum window frames. "I only get 18 cents a pound, but I've done it all my life to have something to do," B.J.'s dad explains. The two of them exist on Medicaid, food stamps, and welfare, which buys the clothes B.J. wears. Though his dad is only forty-nine years old, he seems much older. "They say you're only as old as you feel," he grimaces. "Sometimes I feel real old."[3]

Over thirty years ago, when President Lyndon Johnson declared his war on poverty, he stood on the East Kentucky courthouse steps only sixty miles from where B.J. lives. To date, poverty is winning Johnson's war. According to reporter Guy Gugliotta, this is the land of Daniel Boone, of ancient folklore and handicrafts, and of dulcimers. Great singers have been born and raised here: Jean Ritchie, Loretta Lynn, Crystal Gale, and the Judds, Naomi and Wynonna. But behind the mystery and romance of Appalachia lurks a far different reality. "What we have here is extensive grain alcohol abuse, family violence, homicide, accidents, substance abuse and depression," says Karen Main, the deputy director of the University of Kentucky's Center for Rural Health. "But the real problem is poverty, and we haven't figured out how to treat that."[4]

In Appalachia, most impoverished families are white. Unemployment is 15.2 percent. Only half the adults living here ever got a high-school diploma. Few houses have phones. Most people believe they have only two choices. One is "Greyhound therapy." That means getting on a bus and going somewhere else. The second is staying put, waiting for jobs, and collecting welfare, food stamps, or disability insurance.

Those who decide to stay have little to do but get bored. Boredom leads to drinking. Drinking leads to accidents. All these mountain communities have abnormally high numbers of accidental deaths: people driving off cliffs or into trees. The suicide rate here is also higher than anywhere else in the United States.

URBAN POVERTY

Detroit is a cold city in the winter. In the ghetto known as Black Bottom, water often freezes in the bathroom pipes. Timothy, four, his sister, Regina, age five, had been alone in their apartment for several hours when they decided that standing on a chair close to the gas flame on the kitchen stove might keep them warm. Timothy remembers that his sister was wearing a white dress and that her hair was in braids when she caught fire. The more she flapped her arms to put out the flames, the more the fire spread. Timothy did not know what to do as the white polyester material melted on his sister's body.

When she fell to the floor, he tried hard to put out the flames. He thought that maybe if she could sleep, she'd be okay. She was still breathing when somehow, through a quantum effort, he managed to drag her limp, burned body into bed. No one even knew she was in trouble, for Timothy was afraid he'd done something wrong and wasn't about to cry for help. His sister soon died. For the next several years, until his father moved out, every time he got drunk, he would rage at Timothy: "You killed my daughter!"[5]

In his short life, Timothy experienced the worst of urban horrors. Playing pool at the neighborhood recreation center, he was accidentally shot in the thigh by his older brother. In the next few years, his uncle was shot in the head, two of his older brothers went to prison, and his friends died in car wrecks or were murdered on the streets. At fifteen, his fourteen-year-old girlfriend told him she was having his baby. He wouldn't believe her or take responsibility, and they broke up. He got into drugs. He joined a gang. A few years later when he saw his old girlfriend, he recognized himself in the small boy walking beside her. When he looked at the child, he knew the boy was entering the "same tunnel of horror" he had been caught in since birth.[6]

According to John Dilulio, a Princeton professor:

The problem is that inner-city children are trapped in criminogenic homes, schools, and neighborhoods where high numbers of teenagers and adults are no more likely to nurture, teach, and care for children than they are to expose them to neglect, abuse, and violence. . . . Children cannot be socialized by adults who are themselves unsocialized (or worse), families that exist in name only, schools that do not educate, and neighborhoods in which violent and repeat criminals circulate in and out of jail.[7]

The nation's ghettos are swimming with criminals and drowning in drugs. Families are most often headed by single mothers trying to raise their children alone in neighborhoods too dangerous to venture into after dark. Men hang out at the local bar or on street corners, detached from and uninterested in the lives of their children. Statistically, they will die young, probably violently, or spend at least a portion of their lives in prison. Most of them are black. The little boys playing in the littered alleys or shooting hoops on the asphalt playgrounds will more than likely grow up just like their fathers. The little girls jumping rope on the sidewalks will do what their mothers did—they will get pregnant while they are still in their teens. Then they will have their babies, collect welfare, and repeat the cycle all over again.[8] That is, unless something is done.

FROM MANY AREAS, FROM MANY SITUATIONS

Another way to look at the many faces of welfare is to consider the diverse situations creating the need for welfare. Joanne Brooking, for example, has most of the credits she needs to get a sociology degree from Goddard College in nearby Plainfield, Vermont. Without an additional thirty credit hours needed for her diploma, however, she found it was almost impossible to find a job that paid well enough to support herself and her three young sons after her divorce became final ten years ago. When she found temporary work, substituting in the local schools or selling Amway products, she was no better off, since her welfare check was cut once officials found out she was working. "It isn't that people don't want to work," she says. "It's that there are no jobs out there."[9]

If not divorced, many times families are abandoned by one parent, leaving the other to support the family alone. Most of the time, it is the fathers who leave, the mothers who stay. Sergio, his six brothers and sisters, and his mother were left to fend for themselves in Apopka, Florida. His house caught fire not long ago, spreading so quickly that Sergio was badly burned. His mother had no other place to go, so they moved in with her sister, squeezing into his aunt's little, two-bedroom house. The house itself is squeezed into a neighborhood teeming with crack dealers and addicts.

"These people's problems are overwhelming," one obstetrician tells reporter John McCormick. "I have not fully accepted the fact that, when I come to work [here at the workers' clinic], I am in the United States."[10]

One form of abandonment occurs when a man claims he is not the father of his own child. This used to be a common excuse, but with the DNA testing available today, paternity can be proved through a simple blood test.

Still, getting support is difficult. Some fathers manage to evade paying support by frequently changing jobs. By the time the courts order their paychecks garnished, they have moved on to other work. Other times they manage to get their pay "under the table" and thus without any record of its having been earned. Then, they go into court claiming to have no means to support their children.

Sometimes, even when they don't use any of these ruses, working fathers are literally too poor to pay enough to help much at all. An extreme example of this is the St. Louis soda bottling company worker who had a wife and three legitimate children. When the courts summoned him to pay additional support for the twenty-two out-of-wedlock children he also fathered, the head of child support in St. Louis could only shrug his shoulders: "He's employed, but we can't take any more of his money."[11]

Abandonment has become so common and the costs to welfare to support the children left behind so burdensome that today many states are working overtime to get "deadbeat dads" to pay their fair share of child support. Yet while vast computer data collection systems in some states are making that job easier, irresponsible fathers are still able to escape to other states, out of the local jurisdiction of their penniless families. Until recently, the child-support collection agency of one state has often found the red tape of another state a quagmire not worth fighting. By the time officials in the state of the father's new residence are ready to track him down and serve him with papers, many men move on to safety in another county or state. It takes incredible perseverance and bundles of paperwork to doggedly track these elusive men. Both require a court officer's time, time that few have to spare because their caseloads are far too heavy.

The new welfare reform bill may speed this process. States will now be required to create a central case registry to track the status of all child-support orders created or modified after October 1, 1998. Relevant information will be regularly updated and shared with other computer banks, including a federal case registry. Additionally, states will also establish a "new hire" registry by October 1, 1997. All employers will have to send the names, addresses, and Social Security numbers of newly hired employees, and these will be compared with the child-support registry. When a "new hire" owes child support, the state can order the new employer to withhold wages.

Some families end up on welfare because a parent becomes too ill to work. Other times, a single parent will have to stay home to care for seriously handicapped or ill children. In Detroit, Michigan, Terry Phelan's doctors doubted he would survive his first twenty-four hours. Ten hours after he was born, his head was swollen and misshapen, he was having trouble breathing, and life-support tubes ran from his nose, chest, and arms. Even though he was able to go home a few weeks later, his mother was told that he had cerebral palsy, that he might never walk or talk, and that he was probably mentally retarded.

At twelve months, Terry began butting his head against his crib. By age three, he had to wear a towel and foam mitts fashioned to protect him from hurting himself. Later, he wore a helmet. But even today, when he can manage it, Terry injures himself with terrifying regularity. Sometimes his eyes are swollen shut, his face puffy. His mother often finds his sheets spattered with blood. And still he continues to hit and hit and hit.

For Terry's mother, life offers no alternatives. She knows that Terry needs full-time care. She had a decent job as a bookkeeper, but she cannot find anyone else to take Terry while she works. Nor does she have a car or the money for gas. Although she never dreamed she would have to go on welfare, welfare is Terry's only hope. It is welfare that supports the two of them.[12]

There is yet another type of illness that brings children under the welfare umbrella. It is the sickness created by battery and abuse in their own homes. Children from abusive homes are among the most endangered of all children, because one of their parents not only must be strong enough to protect them from harm, but also often give up home and possessions to do so. Many battered women come to shelters carrying nothing other than a small infant and a few dollars in their wallets. They come having left behind everything they own, knowing that the shelter is perhaps their only hope for survival.

Finally, a growing number of welfare children have

been the products of immigrants who arrived in this country with no assets and no job skills. Some escaped wars; some escaped famine. Many came ill-equipped to adjust easily to their new land. Before coming here from Vietnam, Thaun Chhoeum spent four years with her parents in a refugee camp in Thailand. As an adolescent newly arrived in the United States, Thaun remembers wandering the halls of her new school. "I couldn't read, so I didn't know what room to go in," she explains. She was not to stay very long in school, however, because she had to go to work. Her wages helped her parents raise her six younger brothers and sisters.

Today, Thaun has three children of her own. She is a single parent. Though she receives $900 each month from the state, she still lives in poverty in an apartment directly across the street from her parents. She has finally managed to get her high-school diploma and is now enrolled in a vocational school. She still has trouble with English and with the strangely different ways of her new people.[13]

Immigrants like Thaun will soon feel the knife of new welfare cuts in the welfare reform bill. Legal immigrants will be ineligible for food stamps until they become citizens or until they have worked in the United States for at least ten years. States also will have the option to deny them federal welfare, Medicaid, and other social services. Illegal aliens and legal nonimmigrants such as travelers and students will now be denied most federal benefits except for short-term disaster relief and emergency medical care.

OTHERS ON WELFARE

Only a small percentage of all welfare recipients are chronic welfare abusers. But too often, they are the people who stand out, the ones we remember. Even in welfare neighborhoods, recipients who are abusing the system are scorned:

> A lot of people on welfare are lazy and don't want to look
> for work. A lot of girls keep having kids to get more money
> from welfare. They're usually "fiends" [drug addicts] who
> use the money to buy more drugs and let their kids starve.[14]

Still others continue to produce child after child, without making any effort to become independent. Last year, the *Boston Globe* described the life of Eulalia Rivera, a Puerto Rican who settled in nearby Dorchester, Massachusetts, in the late 1960s. There, she raised seventeen children, all on welfare. Of the seventeen, two live outside the United States, one has died, and the other fourteen, now adults themselves, continue to live on welfare. Between them, they have seventy-four children, and already, those children are having additional children. Eulalia Rivera has single-handedly created a welfare dynasty numbering 103 descendants![15]

THE STATISTICS

While more people live in poverty today, a smaller percentage of them get welfare than those of a generation ago.[16] In 1995, of every seven children in a racially and economically balanced school, one was receiving AFDC. Although that may seem an incredibly high number, even more could be on the welfare rolls if the states were even handed in their distribution of aid, for actually one of every five children lives below the poverty line.[17]

Whites comprise the largest group on welfare. Nearly 40 percent of all people on welfare are white. About 37 percent are black and 18 percent are Hispanics. Only 3 percent are Asian, and another 3 percent are too diverse to characterize. While not quite 60 percent of all people on welfare were in their twenties or older when they gave birth to a child supported by welfare, at present, 5 percent are teenagers, and another 36 percent were teenagers at the time they became parents. More than half, 53 percent, have never married.

Eulalia Rivera's family may send chills down taxpayers' spines, but she is the exception, not the rule. Only 18 percent of all welfare families have three or more children, while a full 84 percent have only one or two. The welfare rolls change constantly, and many welfare recipients go on, then off, then on again more than once. More than half the women receiving aid for their families today will be off the rolls before the year is out. Some will stay off the rolls permanently, but 45 percent will be back before another year passes. Of all those on welfare at this moment, probably a third are working at least part-time, or will work at least temporarily during the year.

These are the real statistics. Research also shows that in a large portion of new welfare families, a parent has recently lost his or her job. To understand why, one has only to read the paper to notice the frequency of companies downsizing their workforces or moving their operations to foreign countries where labor is cheaper and restrictions fewer. "We never meant to quit our jobs," a former Rath meat-packing employee from Waterloo, Iowa, told writer Jacqueline Jones. "They quit on us."[18]

CUTTING THE ROLLS

Clearly, abolishing welfare or doing wholesale cutting of the welfare rolls may not be the best way to approach the welfare problem. The faces of poverty that we saw in the first chapter and the reasons that people find themselves turning to welfare that we have discussed in this chapter should make it obvious that welfare recipients come in every possible shape and size, color and class, and their reasons for needing welfare range widely from extremely worthy to sadly negligible. An interesting way to look at the welfare problem is to consider how much money the chronic welfare recipients, about a quarter of all people on welfare, costs. The 25 percent that stay on welfare for years and years use 60 percent of all the money the government gives out in welfare benefits. They are the most dysfunctional, the hardest to get off welfare. When President Clinton signed HR3734, the bill did not solve this persistent problem. What it actually might do is cut from the rolls "those most likely to leave anyway. . . . Leaving behind a relatively hard core group of recipients."[19]

For the hard core, monthly welfare checks "create a culture of dependency in which children grow up without ever seeing members of their family go to work."[20] Welfare has rewarded what it should have discouraged and has punished what it should have rewarded. Says Ann Clark, a case manager in Colorado Springs, Colorado: "The Federal Government has created a monster. I'm dealing with third-generation recipients. Welfare has become their way of life. It scares them to death to try to get off it."[21] As we shall see in the next chapter, the impact welfare has had on families has all too often been negative. The kinds of families fostered by welfare have changed the meaning of "family" altogether.

FOUR

FAMILY TIES

In St. Francis County, Arkansas, Marquita Kellom lives with her five-month-old baby in a government-housing project and attends Forrest City High School. Marquita has another year of high school to go before she gets her diploma, but she intends to do it. "My mom had me when she was young. She got through it; I'll get through it." Marquita understands what goes through girls' minds at this age. "Eight of my friends want to have babies. They want love, they want to be proud. . . . And about half of them think if they get pregnant by a certain boy, they can get him and keep him."[1]

Marquita knows what she is talking about. When St. Francis County researchers took an anonymous survey of eighty-nine of its unwed mothers, they learned that at least one pregnancy of every five was intentional. Some had "wanted a baby to love who could love [them]," while others said that either their boyfriends wanted them to have a baby or they had believed that "having a baby would give [them] more attention." While a small number of the respondents admitted that they had gotten pregnant to obtain AFDC, most had motives "much more basic than money, much more desperate. . . . For some kids, it's a cry for affection, help, somebody," explained one researcher.[2]

According to the coordinator of health services in Little Rock, Arkansas, Gwen Efrid, "Our nurses see the disappointment on the faces of some girls when they tell them that they're not pregnant. . . . Some of these girls don't see pregnancy as against their interests," says Efrid. "You have to keep reminding them that a baby can only make their lives more difficult."[3] While no one knows for sure just how many girls actually try to get pregnant, some experts think that the figure is well over the 16 percent estimate used by the Centers for Disease Control and Prevention. They also believe that the numbers are growing.

For many other teenagers, pregnancy is a big shock. Tamisha Fields had been having unprotected relations with her boyfriend, Torrey, for more than a year before she got pregnant. "I ain't never had no sex ed classes," she explains. For six months after she got pregnant, she kept it a secret, too frightened to get an abortion because a close friend of hers had died of complications from one.

Today, on the condition that she continues school, Tamisha's parents allow her to stay at home. Their small apartment is crowded. Besides Tamisha, two other young children still live at home. And now there is Torrey, just two, waiting at the window in his Bert and Ernie slippers for his mother to get home from high school. Tamisha is seventeen. She says she'd like to be a nurse. Yet a while ago, Tamisha became pregnant a second time. "I could have killed her, 'cause she knows better now," her mother remembers. Tamisha excuses the second mistake: "Torrey senior doesn't like to wear condoms, and for some reason, the birth-control pills stopped working." Her second child was aborted upon the insistence of her mother: "It was my decision now, okay? If she's going to be here in the house with me, one child is enough until she finishes school."[4]

Marquita Kellom and Tamisha Fields represent a significant portion of the teenage population. The similarities that they share are nothing new. Both girls had mothers who were teenagers when they gave birth; each is doing exactly what her mother did.

Yet other crucial factors are different and new. Writer William Tucker spent much of the late 1960s as a welfare-rights worker in Clark County, Alabama. Even then, most of the older women in the community had given birth to illegitimate children in their teens. But while a young woman who found herself pregnant could expect to be supported by her family, in those days, as the child grew older or as the young woman continued to produce children, the family put intense pressure on her and the father to marry.[5] Most men in the south at that time were farmers, and all worked. Everyone expected young men to marry and support their wives and families, and most did. This pattern of out-of-wedlock births followed by marriage and family, Tucker says, is traceable to Africa and is also seen in immigrants from Puerto Rico and Central America.

Such patterns develop for good reasons. They insure that the society endures. Traditions and institutions are created to protect a society and the individuals in that society. Marriage and family are perhaps the most basic of these institutions, because children must be properly cared for and reared if they are to become the inheritors and guardians of their culture. In *The Family: Past and Present*, Bronislaw Malinowski, considered the first great anthropologist to live among primitive peoples, wrote:

> Through all societies there runs the rule that the father is indispensable for the full sociological status of the child [and] that the group consisting of a woman and her off-

spring is sociologically incomplete and illegitimate. . . . The most important moral and legal rule [in primitive societies] is that no child should be brought into the world without a man—and one man at that—assuming the role of sociological father, that is guardian and protector, the male link between the child and the rest of the community.[6]

WELFARE'S EFFECT ON MARRIAGE AND FAMILY

Many experts believe that welfare policies have been changing the institution of the family. While welfare policies have not caused teenage pregnancy, they have eliminated the financial need for family. In doing so, a complex system of rituals, taboos, expectations, morals, and values that had preserved the family unit was destroyed. Consider this: In 1950, 72 percent of all black men and 81 percent of black women married; only 14 percent of black children were born to unmarried women. Nationally, by 1992, drastic changes had occurred. A majority of black children, 54 percent, now lived in female-headed households and 66 percent of black babies were born out of wedlock. The illegitimacy rate grew to more than 80 percent in some inner-city neighborhoods.[7]

WELFARE AND CHILDBEARING

When young Erica George of Dogwood Acres in Arkansas had her baby two years ago, she received a new rent-free apartment in the projects. She was also granted $162 per month in cash from AFDC, another $206 in food stamps, free health care from Medicaid, and $70 in food vouchers for the baby. One day a gaggle of teenage mothers from the neighborhood sat around her living room, doting on the child. One asked Erica's fifteen-year-old sister Gwen when she was going to get pregnant. She blushed. Someone said, "She'll be having a baby someday soon enough. She's getting to be a big girl." Everyone turned to look at Gwen. Journalist Michael Leahy writes:

> In this moment, the pressure is on a child in a place like Dogwood Acres, a matriarchal society with few men in sight and baby-faced teen-age mothers holding rein. There, to become pregnant and have a child means to be elevated to be something approaching womanhood, graced by a measure of independence, social and financial.[8]

It's not surprising when Gwen replied: "I'm already pregnant." In a study of thirteen thousand teenagers, RAND researchers asked if respondents would consider having an illegitimate child. More than 20 percent of both whites and Hispanics and more than 40 percent of blacks answered "yes" or "maybe."

SINGLE-PARENT FAMILIES

For these girls, and for others who will refuse to entertain the option of abortion or adoption, single parenthood will be filled with obstacles. While most of them cannot or do not want to believe it at the time, single-parent families are disadvantaged in every way. These girls will have a hard time raising their children, especially if they live in crowded urban areas or projects. Such neighborhoods have a high density of children, most of them from similar single-parent households. They foster rebellious peer groups or gangs, groups that have a life of their own, and rules and values of their own. New York senator and welfare expert Daniel Moynihan once warned that a society that allows a large number of young men to grow up without fathers in their lives asks for and gets chaos.[9] As parents in such a setting, single young mothers are hard-pressed to control or discipline their children.

According to Rutgers University professor David Popenoe, single-parent families not only create social problems for their neighborhoods and their society but also increase the child poverty rate by five times that of children living in two-parent families.[10] Additionally, children growing up in such families are two to three times more likely to have emotional and behavioral problems as teenagers.[11] Those who work with these families, the doctors, the social workers, and the police, are dealing with more than what Charles Murray calls "simple poverty." He writes that:

Today's children are too often going malnourished, malnurtured, neglected, and unsocialized, not because their parents have no access to material resources but because the mother is incompetent and the father is missing altogether. Whether the mother's incompetence derives from youth, drug addiction, low ability, an unjust social system, or defective character makes little difference to the child. Even that the mother loves the child makes little difference if the love is unaccompanied by the steadfastness, maturity, and understanding of a child's needs that (turns) love into nurturing.[12]

Yet teenage pregnancy occurs for one of every ten girls, more than a million times each year.[13] While about half will abort, the other half will carry their babies to full term, somehow believing that their lives are going to be different and that they will prove the statisticians wrong.

Families Run by Grandparents

Rose Barrett is a typical example of grandparents who find themselves taking responsibility for their children's children. Rose raised three children of her own as a single mother. Then, through two twists of fate, she found herself starting all over again at age fifty-one. Now she is raising her own granddaughter Shaniqua and her deceased twin sister's three grandsons.

A teenager when her child was born, Shaniqua's mother grew bored with tending her baby and "just wanted to hang out," Mrs. Barrett explains. Finally, they decided it would be better for Shaniqua to live with her grandmother. Shaniqua had no sooner gotten used to her new home than she had to adjust to the arrival of the three boys. The three boys had been in much the same situation with their mother. "They're mostly street kids. They used to cook for themselves, fend for themselves. They're beautiful kids, but I know the life they had in the beginning."[14] When Shaniqua and the three boys came to live with Mrs. Barrett, she had to cut back on her working hours so that she could be home for the children. As a licensed foster mother for the state of New York, she now receives an additional $1400 a month from AFDC and health insurance, which help to make up for her lost income.

THE DAMAGING EFFECTS OF WELFARE

Often, the very behaviors society wishes to eliminate have been fostered by the welfare system. Until 1988, for example, more than half the states in the nation denied a family welfare benefits if the father lived with the family. Such policies harmed children, who benefit from having two parents in the home. Fortunately, the Family Support Act of 1988 required states to let families stay intact yet still receive support.

Until only recently, welfare policies also discouraged working, even part-time, for doing so could jeopardize much needed welfare benefits such as food stamps and health insurance. Consequently, for the children of welfare, a working parent became a rare sight. Experts know that children model their own behaviors on what they see in their homes. If parents don't work, if Daddy hangs out on the local corner or Mommy spends her afternoons watching soap operas, then children grow up believing this is how they should behave.

Additionally, the welfare system has tended to stress punishments: "If you do this, then you will lose your monthly welfare check or food stamps." The "crimes" that are punishable, however, have most often been attempts on the part of recipients to work longer or harder to provide for their children. Hardly ever have families been punished for taking drugs or dropping out of high school. This may change with the new welfare reform legislation, which allows states to deny welfare to those convicted of a felony offense for possession, use, or distribution of an illegal drug. Yet welfare has few or no provisions for rewarding positive behavior such as keeping children in school, getting regular health checkups, or participating in school-support programs, all of which are healthy signs that recipients are taking responsibility for themselves, their children, and their community.

WELFARE DEPENDENCY

According to most research studies, the old myth that one generation of welfare recipients creates successive welfare generations is unfounded. The experts say that four of five children from a welfare-dependent family will likely get jobs when they become adults. Only one is likely to stay on welfare. Other studies have shown that welfare children are no more likely to require welfare assistance later in life than are other poor children.[15]

Yet examples of welfare dependency perpetuated by welfare dependency abound. Today, unlike any other time in history, parents can bear children without taking financial responsibility for them, and an entire subculture has developed because of it.[16] In some places, welfare has created a "subculture" of recipients whose values, beliefs, sexual mores, and economy are quite different from and in some ways actually opposed to society as a whole.

In such subcultures, teenage mothers who have already had a child or two are likely to accuse friends who are still childless of "thinking you're better than us."[17] To wait until one is twenty-five or thirty to have a child is considered "spinsterish" or "weird." Yet in mainstream society, twenty-five to thirty is the time most couples choose for child rearing; they delay in order to have enough money to raise their families.

University of Pennsylvania professor Elijah Anderson thinks that males have had to find other ways to build self-esteem, including making babies to prove their manhood. A sense of responsibility for those children, however, is missing. When Professor Anderson asked why they did not marry their girlfriends, they said, "Because I can't play house," meaning they did not have a job that allowed them to support a family.[18]

Some young men even encourage their girlfriends to have babies so that they can share the payments their girlfriends receive from welfare. The girl "lives home with Mom and Dad, and the $158 she gets every two weeks amounts to an allowance. She gives a lot of it to the boy."[19] This practice has become so commonplace that many young men actually expect their "fair share" of the welfare checks when their girlfriends receive them, saying "If it weren't for me, you wouldn't be getting this check."[20]

In welfare subcultures, teenage fathers of multiple children have no problem refusing to take legal responsibility for their offspring. They "express horror at the possibility of marriage" and claim "they wouldn't begin to consider it until [they're] at least thirty."[21] When politicians talk about getting welfare mothers to work, not much is said at all about getting welfare fathers to admit paternity or to contribute to the family income by going to work themselves.

Society's Response

Changes in family structure have forced society to take a new look at what it expects the family to be and to do, especially with regard to children. The alarming statistics on teenage and other out-of-wedlock pregnancies and on single-parent families receiving welfare seem to go hand in hand with other alarming statistics on drugs, violence, and crime.

Society's response has taken three directions. One has been to preserve the family at all costs, using various child-care programs and counseling groups to help endangered families stay together. The second direction has been to promote foster care as a way of protecting children whose parents have proved incapable, irresponsible, or negligent. The third direction has been to propose developing a system of orphanages for impoverished children. These would replace welfare as we know it.

Foster Care

Until the mid-1970s, the primary means of caring for children from negligent or abusive homes was the foster-care system. The goal of foster care was to provide temporary homes for children whose parents were experiencing problems that interfered with their ability to properly care for their children, who were impoverished and homeless, or who were too young to support children. Foster care was considered temporary in that authorities fully expected to return the children to their parents as soon as they were able to care for them themselves.

While the foster-care system was intended to be a temporary solution to the problem of child protection, it had problems. Children voluntarily given up to foster care or children that the courts forcibly withdrew from their birth homes often remained in a state of limbo, sometimes for years on end, because their parents were unwilling to give them up for adoption but unable to take them home again. Many of these long-term children were uprooted from one foster home to another if they didn't fit in, if the foster family's circumstances changed, or if a social worker decided that moving the child was in his or her best interests.

When it was first begun, foster care made a great deal of sense. If parents were too young or too poor to adequately care for their children, the state was able to find temporary homes where children could thrive. That was at a time when mothers tended to stay home. A large pool of women were available to take in foster care children. In addition, while some children most certainly came from abusive homes, many more did not. They tended to be relatively normal youngsters who could fit in easily with their new families.

That was before the majority of married women began working outside the home. Today, the pool of available foster mothers has shrunk dramatically. In addition, since that time, child-abuse cases have more than doubled, an epidemic of children are being born drug-addicted, and diseases such as AIDS are being transferred to unborn children. These are children with serious problems. While many parents are willing to exert the extra effort that problem children require, many more are not emotionally or physically equipped to do so.

Today, the foster-care system cares for more than one-half million children. Another half million are in detention centers or correctional institutions. The system is overburdened, underfunded, and inefficient, and it is constantly subject to criticism from all sides. Horror stories abound of children who have been subject to physical or sexual abuse while in foster care. Every state has its cases of children who have died or who have been murdered while in foster care, as well. The foster care system is expensive and difficult to manage, and it cannot guarantee that all children will be protected while under its auspices. Until the late 1970s, however, it was the only alternative the government had.

FAMILY PRESERVATION

In the mid-1970s, social workers in Tacoma, Washington, proposed a grant for a "super foster home" facility that would teach foster parents how to cope with their increasingly difficult charges. The National Institute of Mental Health studied the proposal and responded by asking why such counseling and educational services shouldn't be offered instead to the birth families of these difficult children. Doing so, they said, could eliminate the need for foster care altogether. That is how the "family preservation" movement came into being.

Family preservation's aim to decrease the number of children requiring foster care was based on several assumptions. The first was that it is better to keep children at home and help the family deal with the trauma causing the problem than to expose children to the greater trauma of loss of home and parent(s). The second assumption was that short-term intense intervention by counselors, free food, cash, furniture, rent vouchers, and child-care help could turn most poor parents into good parents. The third assumption was that the definition of "family" was far too narrow; practically any cluster of people living together, permanently or temporarily, constituted a family.

The family preservation concept spread across the nation within a few short years. The federal government passed the Adoption Assistance and Child Welfare Act of 1980 that required all states to make "reasonable efforts" to prevent foster-care placements and to hasten return of children to their birth families. But it was in the mid- to late-1980s that family preservation became the byword of nearly every social-service agency. By then, the crack epidemic had hit every sector of society, and child abuse and neglect cases had doubled. Child welfare costs spiraled, and politicians and government agencies knew that something had to be done to stop them. Suddenly, family preservation became the cure for every domestic ill. Bill Moyers ran a TV special describing its value. A national clearinghouse was set up so that every jurisdiction could get information on it. Presidential advisors touted it; the Michigan Department of Social Services testified to its effectiveness.

Family preservation has not, however, proved to be the miracle cure many hoped it would be. It cannot solve the family's problems today, because the families in need of help are too seriously damaged. As one expert explained it, the families it serves are:

> characterized by . . . substance abuse and a weakened extended family. . . . [It] possesses pervasive emotional and behavioral problems and is crippled in its abilities to compete in society. Such families are firmly set in a downward spiral; their problems seem to defy all notions of a "quick fix."[22]

While the foster-care system has its share of horror stories, the family-preservation movement may soon overtake it. Since the program began in 1988 in Illinois, six children have died violent deaths during preservation counseling or just after.[23]

Such was the case of Saonnia B. Saonnia's aunt reported that the three-year-old girl had been abused by both her mother and her mother's boyfriend. Social workers responded by visiting and counseling the family for four months, making thirty-seven visits to the home. A case-worker shopped with Saonnia's mother, Sadie, for shoes and furniture and evaluated Sadie's cooking, housekeeping, and budgeting. Then they closed the case, reporting that the family was much improved. "The amount of stress and frustration has been reduced. Sadie appears to have a lot more patience with her children and she continues to improve her disciplinary techniques," the worker wrote.[24] Unfortunately, practically before the case could be filed, Saonnia was dead. In the emergency room, doctors found forty-three scars and burns on her body from wounds most likely inflicted during the family-preservation counseling.

After investigating a similar wrongful death, the panel in charge wrote: "It would be comforting to believe that the facts of this case are so exceptional that such cases are not likely to happen again, but . . . that hope is unfounded."[25] Another expert, Robert Halpern, a professor of child development at the Erikson Institute in Chicago, points out that even if these children survive their horrific childhood homes, they will grow up so emotionally and psychologically damaged that no one will ever be able to help them. "The danger is not just the enormous damage to the kid himself, but producing the next generation of monsters."[26]

ORPHANAGES

If social-service agencies can't find enough decent foster homes for children and if parents can't be trusted to bring them up, the problem of what to do with parentless children becomes enormous. The third direction policymakers have considered is a system of orphanages. Today churches and private charities operate the majority of group homes, our modern-day equivalent to the orphanage. A group home may have as few as four children, a residential treatment center as many as a hundred or more, housed in clusters of eight to twelve. These group homes or residential clusters are always supervised by full-time house parents and child-care personnel, many of whom actually live on the premises. Most are not meant to be a long-term solution for the child. After a few months or years, the child is returned to his or her birth home, adopted, or placed in foster care. Older youngsters often graduate to less restrictive group homes or to their own rooms or apartments while still under the limited supervision of child welfare.

Most experts agree that the children now in residential treatment programs are very different from orphans of only a few decades ago. They tend to distrust adults, they cannot tolerate family life, and their behavior is too disruptive for them to remain in public school. Twenty years ago, the typical response to the stock psychiatrists' question, "If you had three wishes, what would they be?" would have been "I want a basketball" or "I wish my father didn't drink." Today, explains director Nan Dale of the Children's Village, one more likely hears: "I wish I had a gun so I could blow my father's head off."[27]

Approximately 16 percent of all children under the auspices of child welfare, more than sixty-five thousand young people, are in group homes and residential treatment centers. Centers are overwhelmed with applicants. Boys Town of Omaha, Nebraska, turns down eight to nine applicants for every one child it admits.[28] It is the same everywhere. Unfortunately, the only way to keep up with the numbers in need of homes is to increase the number and size of the centers. Children get lost in such systems. In addition, the costs of housing and educating a child can range between $40,000 and $48,000 a year. The total cost could be in the billions. Taxpayers are not likely to be happy about this third alternative.

The Face of the Family

Fifty years ago, the definition of the word *family* was clear to everyone, but today this is not the case. While once the family was considered "the original and best department of health, education, and welfare,"[29] today drugs, teenage and out-of-wedlock pregnancies, and growing dependency on the government have weakened the family. No one knows how to make the family strong again. No one knows whether all families should be strengthened or whether some are better off dissolved. And as always, there is the recurring question of what happens to the children?

As we shall see in the next several chapters, there is no simple solution. Whether together or apart, families in need of public welfare suffer from lack of decent housing, good health and nutrition, and proper education. These problems increase stress on families and make preserving them even more difficult.

FIVE

HOME SWEET HOME

In California, Sandra ponders the loss of an old dream. She and her girlfriends used to spend their afternoons fantasizing about going to the same college, renting an apartment, and living together. They liked to think about life, being young and free, going to classes, going to parties and athletic events, meeting cute boys who would be someone, who would get good jobs and make a decent living. Now she smiles, then shrugs. "No more of that," she says, knowing those dreams are gone forever.[1]

Sandra's boyfriend and the father of her child is seventeen. He has his General Education Degree (GED) and he works, but he doesn't earn enough to pay for a place for the three of them. He lives with his family; Sandra and baby Angelica live with hers. "It's better to live at home because when he's around, we argue. Sometimes I call him on the phone if I get grumpy, if Angelica cries a lot, and I say, 'Pick her up and take her away.'"

In many ways, Sandra is better off than many. Her parents allow her to live at home, and they plan to let Sandra remain in their house when they retire to Fresno, California.

Sandra has been getting $535 a month from AFDC and an additional $85 in food stamps, so she is surviving rather easily. On the other hand, many teenage mothers find themselves homeless because their parents can't or won't continue to support them. "Some have been kicked out. . . . They move from house to house, friend to friend," explains a teenage pregnancy and parenting nurse. One of her clients moved five times in six months.[2]

While Angelica is getting a relatively good start in life, other children are living in the meanest of environments. These range from "urban campgrounds" housing dozens of homeless families to projects that are dangerous and degrading. Not many miles away from Sandra and her baby, Chris Benton, age four, keeps asking his mother, "We aren't going to live here forever, are we? When are we going home?"[3] Despite his young age, Chris knows that they aren't camping, a lie the adults at the campground tell their uprooted children. The campground is filled with tents and blankets. It is surrounded by a chain-link fence and is situated beside a railroad track. Camping is supposed to be fun, but living here isn't.

While Angelica sleeps in her crib, across the nation other children like Chris accompany their unemployed mothers and fathers wherever they go: looking for jobs, waiting in welfare agencies, eating in soup kitchens, sleeping in cars or in makeshift tents. Some sleep in public shelters; others sleep in welfare motels or high-rise welfare hotels; still others sleep in projects where, commonly, the sound of sporadic gunfire long ago replaced the nighttime cooing of pigeons or the sounds of tree frogs. All of them yearn for a safe place they can call home, but none of them have much control over whether or not they will get it. The control is in the hands of state and local government agencies overwhelmed and overburdened with people who have no jobs, no food, and most desperately, no place to sleep.

Two of every three children whose family income falls below the poverty line live in buildings owned by private individuals or groups. Much of it is substandard housing because it does not meet basic safety and sanitary codes. Substandard housing in the price range of most welfare recipients and the working poor can be anything from cellars, garages, dilapidated tenements to tool sheds and chicken coops. In Los Angeles, the *Times* claims two hundred thousand people, mostly families, are so desperate for housing within their price range that they are living in forty-two thousand of the city's garages.[4] Three generations of the Gonzalez family pay nearly five hundred dollars for such a dwelling. Exposed electrical wires run along the unfinished walls. The baby plays on the linoleum-over-concrete floor.

In the Southwest, another form of private housing called colonias has spread throughout the lower Rio Grande valley in Texas. Colonias are rural subdivisions that rival the worst Appalachia has to offer for loathsome living conditions. Ten children from one family live in a "cramped, dark and drafty three-room shack."[5] They have no heat and no septic system. When it rains, the roads and yards around their shack are flooded with raw sewage. On such days, the children wade through this muck to get to school. More than 250,000 people live here; half the adults are unemployed. When the water company turned off Roberto Costilla's family's water because they could not pay their bill, his mother began filling ten-gallon buckets of water at a neighbor's house so they could have drinking water, bathe themselves, and wash their dishes. Soon after, both Roberto and his dad became mysteriously ill with open sores on their faces and arms. The source of the problem was their drinking water. It was contaminated with human feces.[6]

Urban areas are equally bad. People are warehoused in

crumbling rooms that often have no stove or refrigerator. Their plumbing may or may not work, and the heat often goes off during the coldest months of the year. Many of these buildings are unfit for human habitation. They are lice infested, they are thick with coats of lead paint, their wiring is loose and frayed, they are filthy, they are unsound, and those who live in them do so unprotected by fire alarms or sprinklers. They are disasters waiting to happen, yet they are sought by the poor because there is nothing else available.

Because these areas are littered with garbage, rats and roaches infest the walls and other dark, dank places where they breed unbothered. One day, Jessica's mother Margarita opened the living-room door and saw several one-foot rats running here and there from sofa to chair. Knowing she could do little about the problem, she managed to ignore it until finally, one night she found a rat in her baby's crib. The rat was after the milk in the baby's bottle. The whole incident so frightened the family that Margarita, Jessica, and even her little brother Christopher spent the next several nights guarding the baby. Meanwhile, she called the City Health Department. When health workers investigated, they ordered everyone out of the tenement. With no place to go, Jessica and her family had to stay in a public shelter until they found another place to live.[7]

Public Shelters

When shelter in private housing is lost through illness, a change in welfare benefits, fire, or sale of the property, the families who live in them face grave difficulties. In *Rachel and Her Children*, writer Jonathan Kozol details the steps such a family must take to find a home. First, if they are already out on the street, they find the nearest Income Maintenance (welfare) Center. There the children wait with their parents for as long as it takes to find out where to go next. That wait can be all day. If the center has no shelter available for them before dark, they will be told to go to an Emergency Assistance Unit (EAU). The EAU will then assign the family to one of two types of shelters: a barracks shelter or a welfare hotel.

At the barracks shelter, exhausted parents and children will be led into a vast room filled with cots spaced three-feet apart. If a child has to get up during the night to go to the bathroom, parents find themselves warily picking their way through a labyrinth of sleeping strangers.

To make a "place" for themselves, most families pull all their cots together, put a crib at the end, and perhaps drape a blanket over its outer rail to provide at least a semblance of privacy. But privacy is impossible. They are, after all, in a huge room. "There are always some eyes looking at you. You might think nobody is looking at you, but they're looking. It makes you kind of paranoid. Everybody's watching you put your socks on," said one shelter child.[8] Not only are families scrutinized, but everything they say is heard by someone else. And if children are running around, crying or fighting, even playing, the noise can be overwhelming.

Because these shelters are temporary, with people coming and going nightly, the living conditions are poor if not downright unhealthy. Mattresses and pillows are slept on by different people each night. One teenage girl whose family was placed temporarily in a hotel called the Prospect in the Bronx, New York, told author Judith Berck, "It was awful. There was a hole in the wall big enough for a person to walk through. There was blood on the sheets and bugs on the soap. All we could do was throw a blanket over the top of the wall to cover the hole, and we slept there because it was too late to go somewhere else."[9] Some facilities are in worse condition than others, but few families in need of public shelter are likely to have been able to maintain proper personal hygiene. Thus lice are common.

So are mice. Eunice Rodriguez, her husband, and her baby had been in a New York City shelter for just a few days before she noticed mouse turds among her baby's blankets. Eunice tried to protect the child by sleeping next to her, but the mice got the next best thing: the child's new snowsuit. They gnawed and shredded the cuffs. Ms. Rodriguez said, "There must have been some food stuck on them and when I put it in the locker, the mice came and just chewed the cuffs up. What am I supposed to do?"[10]

Certainly, not all shelters are bad. Many privately run shelters do a far better job of providing for needy people than the government-funded shelters do. But for the poor, shelter living is about as stressful as life can be, and always uppermost in everyone's minds is the fact that it is temporary. Tomorrow or the next day or the next, someone may decide the family must be moved elsewhere.

While shelter nights are probably the hardest to accept, days are not much easier. Shelter children who are old enough to be in school may get up in the morning and head for school, but the younger children will have to go with their parents back to the welfare center. The family must be sure that the center has their new address, or they could lose their welfare benefits. Each day they also hope that the EAU worker is going to have something better for them, perhaps even a short-term hotel. At a short-term hotel, the family might have its own bathroom and a place to sleep that is all their own. They may even be able to stay for a few days before they have to go back to the EAU for a new assignment.

Families caught in this system know that the most they can hope for is a permanent assignment, a place of their own where the children will get a chance to make some friends. Most are bitterly disappointed because the "shelter-EAU-short-term-hotel" cycle can continue for months, even years. Families can be sent anywhere in the city, for any amount of time, and they are seldom given any sense of when they might hope for a permanent place.

WELFARE HOTELS

When finally they are placed in long-term welfare hotels in New York City and others like it, the relief children and parents feel will be only temporary. New York City has sixty or more welfare hotels; three of them house more than one thousand families.[11] The apartments are decaying and dirty. A typical unit that costs welfare $3,000 a month to rent has crumbling walls, cracked or missing bathroom tiles, and often a broken toilet. The rooms usually reek of urine and mildew. Ceiling leaks drip into pails. Lead levels in these hotels are usually well above the legal limit. Garbage accumulates in hallways, bins, and littered alleys. Adequate security is too costly, so muggings and other crimes are common. When security is provided, the neighborhoods are often so dangerous that even armed guards are attacked. One young girl in New York explained: "My mother is afraid to let me go downstairs. Only this Saturday the security guard at the hotel was killed on my floor. . . . People are afraid to open the door to even look out. I once found needles and other things that drugs come in in the hallway."[12] And guards can often be bribed:

> I felt like I was never safe. Nobody was, really. It was the management's fault people were getting in. If you wanted to do drugs upstairs and you didn't want anybody bothering you, you gave the security guard five dollars. You could go

upstairs and no one would know. Dealers would come in to count their crack, or store their goods, or whatever it was they needed at the time.[13]

Conditions in suburban areas aren't much better. In Westchester County, just outside New York City, more than forty motels are now being used to house welfare recipients. Like their city counterparts, these motels are often drug dens, rife with crime, and certainly unsafe for children. For example, people who live in the Elmsford Motor Lodge (in Westchester) say more than 80 percent of the residents use crack, reports Brad Kessler in the *Nation*.[14] One resident told him that most drug abuse begins after arriving at the motel: "You get people coming in here that are so nice at the beginning, but by the time they leave here, they're drug addicts or they're so bitter because this place just makes them crazy."[15]

Barbara Jones and her three boys live in a cramped, one-room welfare unit at the Norwalk-Westport Motel, in Norwalk, Connecticut. The family has managed to cram most of their belongings into the one bureau the motel provides, but the rest they leave in plastic bags in the corner. "I'm hoping to land a rental through Section 8 (a federal housing subsidy program), but I know I'm way down on the list," she told the *Fairpress*.[16]

Jo, another welfare recipient willing only to use her first name for fear of her abusive ex-husband, returned to Connecticut after he tried to kill her. She was pregnant at the time. "I feel like I have no choices," says Jo, who has been receiving AFDC. Recent welfare cuts in Connecticut meant that last month Jo and her baby daughter received $70 less than the month before. Because of Connecticut's welfare reforms, she has twenty-one months before she loses her welfare benefits altogether.

Jo tried to find low-income housing only to discover the

waiting list is several years. Day after day, she combed through newspaper ads and drove around looking for an apartment whose owner would accept her Section 8 certificate. But Fairfield County, Connecticut, is an area where the average rent for a one-bedroom unit is eight hundred fifty dollars to nine hundred dollars. Even with every kind of welfare grant available, Jo cannot afford to pay a price this high.[17]

In most suburban motels, people feel isolated. They have little to do and nowhere to go. For the most part, they stay in their rooms, venturing out only to the grocery store. Children have no yard, no side street on which to ride a bicycle, literally no place to play. They have no sense of neighborhood, and they know better than to try to look for friends, because life in these places is only temporary.

THE PROJECTS AND LOW-INCOME HOUSING

One-third of all welfare children live in federally assisted housing. The waiting lists for subsidized housing of this sort in some areas of the country can be so long that children might grow up before the family's name comes up on the list. The length of the list, however, has nothing to do with the desirability of the dwellings. Most projects are rife with crime and often frightening places to live. Buildings are scarred with graffiti and filth. Windows are shattered by stray bullets. Gangs lurk in the stairwells and doorways.

Outside Ella Renfro's Stateway Gardens apartment window in Chicago, a thirteen-year-old boy was killed. Her children could not understand how that could happen, and Ella had no way to make sense of it either. She would love to move away, but she only makes $265 a week, and subsidized housing is the best she can afford. "If I could have a stable job and money and secure myself, yes, I would leave. I would find a place where we could have peace of mind, where I could let my kids play. . . . You would not have to see guns under your face." But she cannot afford better, so she stays. She has lived in this complex for twenty of her thirty-three years. During that time, she has been on and off welfare numerous times. Now that she has a job, even though it pays almost nothing, she is trying to save a few dollars a week so that someday, things might be different. "People think you have nothing, you don't want nothing," she says softly. "Everybody wants to get out and do a little bit better."[18]

The Effects of Poor Housing

Several years ago, educator and lecturer Robert Coles wrote about the lives of children caught in the mire of poverty, homelessness, and public shelters. The article was called "Lost Youth," and in it, Coles quoted a five-year-old girl's question to her mother: "How many times will we have to move until we stop?" she asked. Her mother did not or could not reply. Finally the small girl said, "Only when we find a home can we catch our breath."[19] In that same article, Coles cited a sixth-grade girl who told him: "Someday, we might get a place to live, where we can stay put. . . . You're not wandering anymore. You can unpack, and discover where all you own is—the stuff you've been carrying around. You can be yourself, and not someone waiting for the time to pass until you have your own place."[20]

SIX

FAILURE TO THRIVE

For children to thrive, certain conditions must exist. First, parents must provide for children's well-being so that they have the emotional stability to survive. Literally every child-care expert agrees that children are healthiest when they have parents who are there for them to care for them, to teach them how to get along, and to model behavior the children can imitate to "fit" into society.

Second, children must have a place that is clean and warm, safe and secure that they call home. It must be permanent or as close to permanent as possible, because children too often uprooted frequently suffer undue losses.

Third, children must be given the opportunities to grow physically and intellectually. They must be provided with proper nutrition and be carefully monitored by their pediatricians for good health.

Failure to thrive is a medical term that doctors use to describe children who are not developing normally because of malnutrition or other factors. But failure to thrive can also be used loosely to describe many of the children of welfare because they experience deprivations that undermine their emotional, physical, and intellectual growth. In prior chapters we have seen how unstable family structures and poor living conditions affect welfare children. This chapter considers the physical and intellectual problems caused by poverty because their impact is equally important to child development.

NUTRITION

Georgette Lacy, a Chicago welfare mother, knows of two boys up the hall who scavenge for food in her building's garbage incinerator. They are only three and five, but their mother has left them no choice. "[She] is strung out on rock cocaine," Lacy says.[1]

Stephanie Lambert, age ten, looks forward to getting up in the morning because she knows that waiting for her in the school cafeteria is a cup of juice, Frosted Flakes, milk, toast, and a fried "breakfast bar" of potatoes, ham, and egg. That is probably the best meal she is going to eat all day. Her family has no such luxuries at home, so if she is late for school, she knows that she will pay dearly for the rest of the day: "I don't feel like doing my work. I get a headache and my stomach starts hurting."[2]

In Baltimore, the cafeteria workers worry when school is closed too many times on snow days. "We're sure the children aren't eating well," one says. "The day the children [come] back to school, breakfast [is] like, 'Give me something to eat!'"[3]

While hunger is a greater problem today than it was twenty-five years ago, barely half the people eligible for food stamps are getting any.[4] A little more than a year ago, a new study on hunger in America showed that twenty-five million Americans, most of them under seventeen years of age, were using food pantries, soup kitchens, and other food distribution programs to survive. "People don't have the money to pay the rent and the heating bills and buy food," says the director of one food relief program.[5] When push comes to shove, they go hungry rather than lose their homes.

Some experts question these statistics. They say that food stamps are available to those who need them. Although some of the poor may occasionally visit a food bank, they don't need to do so regularly. These experts believe that people must be abusing the system. "The more programs you have that hand out food for free, the more people will use them," they say.

To prove their position, experts point to people like Theresa, a welfare mother of four in Massachusetts. Theresa has learned how to manipulate the system so well that her children have food left over to feed the birds. "I'm street smart," she says. She has faked residence in several neighboring towns, including Lynn and Salem, Massachusetts, so she can use multiple sources to get food. She also knows who gives out what, and goes from place to place picking up such things as fresh bread on Mondays from St. Mary's Church then carrots and escarole at the food bank to feed their pet iguana.[6]

Whether as many as twenty-five million go hungry or not, too many families are hard pressed to provide proper diets for their growing children. Easter and Nathaniel Williams live in Chicago with their ten children. They have found several ways to deal with the habitual food shortages they experience around midmonth. That's when their food stamps run out. "You start letting everyone sleep late. Then you can combine breakfast and lunch." They have also learned how to minimize hunger after dinner. "The trick is to feed them late with a lot of water and then put them to bed."[7] When all else fails, both parents and the older children skip meals so that the younger ones have something to eat.

In "Poverty's Legacy—Fragile Families, Vulnerable Babies," writer Marilyn Gardner describes the waiting room at Boston City Hospital in Massachusetts. This is a failure-to-thrive clinic that services malnourished children. When a child fails to thrive, the child's life is in danger. Most of the children here have failed to gain the normal amount of weight they should. Some have been given a diet of diluted formula or nondairy creamer in their bottles, because their mothers cannot pay for milk. Toddlers often eat the cheapest foods their parents can get them, even though these foods do not meet nutritional requirements for good health. The effect is astonishing. Some of the giggling children who look like toddlers two or three years of age aren't toddlers at all. Some are six and seven years old.[8]

Even when families have enough food stamps to obtain food, they risk eviction if they try to cook on illegal hot plates in their temporary shelters or welfare hotels. When they do take such risks, they cannot worry about balancing diets. They tend to eat canned goods and other nonperishable items because they have no refrigerator to store food. The food is cooked one type at a time, so it must be an easy and quick recipe. Children sit on the floor or balance their plates on the bed, certainly an ungainly way to eat. And finally, the bathtub serves as the kitchen sink where dishes are washed.

Those who do not have food to eat, who run out of food stamps too early in the month, or who dare not cook in their present quarters must often eat in soup kitchens. Eileen, thirteen, and her mother from Lynn, Massachusetts, are embarrassed to have sunk so low. They are fearful of being forced to eat "with bums." Less than a year ago, Eileen's mother had a job that paid $42,000 a year as a hospital lab technician. Now she has no job. They had lived in a handsome apartment. Now they have a public-housing apartment. They get $130 in food coupons, but it is not enough to make it the entire month, especially if Eileen has friends visit after school. She has to give them something for a snack. "It's very humiliating," her mother says. Tonight Eileen just can't make herself eat all of her chop suey and jello. When she pushes her plate away, her mother grows frantic. She knows if she doesn't eat heartily now, Eileen will most certainly be hungry later. Later, there will be nothing in the house. "Next time you have to make sure you eat every drop," she snaps.[9]

The people who eat in food kitchens are grateful for what they get. Yet they can't escape feeling somehow degraded by the lining up, getting a number, being dealt one serving. "You can always tell the family . . . that's new," one priest told Jonathan Kozol. "Their heads are always down. . . . They eat very quickly and then they disappear."[10]

HEALTH

Good diet is inextricably connected to health, and in many sections of the United States, health care is poor or nonexistent. In Appalachia, they call it "poverty's trailer," the kind of catastrophe that follows poverty wherever it goes. "People are poor, so nobody wants to treat them, and when they do get treated, it is either too late, very expensive, or both," explains one doctor.[11]

One-fourth of all pregnant women in the United States receive little or no prenatal care.[12] Because problems aren't discovered early enough, the United States lags behind eighteen other nations in infant mortality. A study in Boston found that 14 percent of inner-city children were born below birth weight.[13] That is three times the normal rate. Some pregnant women are too overwhelmed with other problems such as substance abuse to take much care of themselves. More are frustrated by the obstacles. One eighteen-year old mother staying at Covenant House in New York explained:

"I had to take four buses just to get to the clinic. If the buses were late and I missed my appointment, I had to come back another day."[14]

The numbers of welfare children affected by Medicaid cuts in the last decade are staggering. Hundreds of community health-care centers that depended on government funding have been permanently shut down. In poor areas, doctors can't make enough money to survive. The ones who do stay are thinned out over a large geographic areas. Poor families in rural areas most often have to use hospital emergency rooms or ambulatory clinics, but getting children to one that will accept them can mean an epic journey, entailing hours and miles of driving.

"People say, 'Get your kid to the doctor,' not knowing that may be the last thing on your list," Tammie Hughes says. "Not that an ear problem isn't important. But food and a place to live always have to come first."[15]

Because living poor can often mean frequent moves, health care suffers even more. Pediatricians have to be changed with every move, and health records often get lost in the shuffle. Consequently, doctors seeing children for the first time are forced to make diagnoses on the basis of sketchy health backgrounds. Following through on continued visits or on necessary medications afterward is often forgotten in the turmoil of lives lived in poverty.

In Appalachian Kentucky, the incidence of cervical cancer, one of the easiest of all cancers to detect and control, is twice as high, because women just can't get regular PAP smears. Preventive health care services such as immunizations and screening for hypertension and diabetes could save a lot of lives, but instead people wait for the stabbing pain of a heart attack or some other full-blown crisis before getting help.[16]

Whether rural or urban, poor people are covered by Medicare or Medicaid, or they have no insurance at all.

Either way, health care is among their lowest priorities, because reimbursement for medical service is only partial or nonexistent.

Consequently, in the physical development of welfare children, all too many problems occur. From conception through adulthood, many welfare children will never know what it is to live on a healthy diet—how good it feels to eat all that they want at dinner, how good it feels to have energy, how good it feels to have the staying power to pay attention in school or to play ball all day. And then, when their bodies suffer for lack of good nutrition or when illness strikes because they are not in good physical condition, all too often their parents will wait too long to see a doctor.

Proper nutrition and regular health care are taken for granted by middle-class and upper-class children. They can be whisked to the doctor on a moment's notice for the slightest discomfort or irregularity. Welfare children and children of the working poor will be lucky if they get to see a doctor at all. While an untreated toothache might cause mild discomfort, an untreated stomachache, unnoticed sweating, or unheeded lumps may be symptoms of an illness that can end their days before they've ever had a chance to live.

SEVEN

UNEQUAL EDUCATION

In cities such as Chicago, as many as 5,700 children come to school on any given day only to find they have no teacher.[1] When a school system does not have enough funds to pay substitutes, students have to sit in unattended classes or be sent on their way. "We've been in this typing class a whole semester," said one fifteen-year-old from Du Sable High, "and they still can't find us a teacher."

In a Chicago elementary school, little Keisha ignores the adult at the front of the classroom who is yelling for her attention. Keisha needs the crayon that her classmate is using, and she's ready to fight for it, because crayons are in great demand. Her city can't afford to buy new ones, so supplies have to be rationed.[2] But to Keisha, whose drawing needs the color red, that explanation means nothing.

In Cincinnati, school teacher Kris Weaver spent July scraping the peeling paint off his Rothenberg Elementary classroom walls so that he could apply a fresh coat. Although the Cincinnati school system does have a painting crew, its size has been reduced from forty to three. Three men cannot maintain the eighty-four schools in the district.

"It gets really bad. The paint just flakes off. The windows are even worse," Weaver says, pointing to the gap of more than one-half inch between the sills and the wooden ledges. Cincinnati gets very cold in the winter. The wind whips around the buildings day after day. But with these windows, it also whips into Kris's classroom. "Ninety-nine percent of the kids in this school are on welfare," he says. "This is their only real safe haven. It's supposed to be nice, but it's falling apart."[3]

Rothenberg was once an extraordinary school. It had a swimming pool in the basement and a playground on the roof. Entryways carved with stone owls and lions made it seem more a cathedral of learning than a mere public school. It made its students believe that education was the finest and most important thing in the world. Today, the city's attitude toward education seems quite a different thing. Principal Patricia Torrey remembers her first impression of Rothenberg when she arrived there more than five years ago: "The floor was permeated with urine. . . . The toilets were leaking. There were no doors on the stalls. It was dark and dingy, and the walls were filthy." Students also see the deterioration of this place. "I feel embarrassed," one fourth grader said. "[Plaster and pieces of paint] kept falling on our heads. We got it all over our hands. It was bad."[4]

Rothenberg is typical of what has happened to most urban and many rural schools as well in virtually every state and county in the nation. They have become "monuments to neglect" that are anything but safe learning environments. In the District of Columbia, a federal judge wants to prevent the schools from opening in the fall until the system corrects at least 1,807 of its 4,000 fire code violations. In New Orleans, all but a few of the 125 schools are not handicap accessible, 54 lack air-conditioning, and 72 need extensive electrical repair. In New York City, teachers and parents recently joined together in a legal suit to force the city to pay $1 billion in repairs, ranging from falling plaster ceilings to leaking roofs.[5]

In classrooms across the nation, especially in urban classrooms, children are packed in, desks crowded together, and teachers overwhelmed by a sea of faces because there are not enough funds to keep class size within reasonable limits. In classrooms so crowded, discipline inevitably suffers. Lessons are forgotten, and nobody learns much of anything except that to be bad at least gets you some attention.

For poor children, dreams of becoming a scientist or a computer specialist are hard to nurture when they never have a chance to do interesting experiments in hands-on laboratories or when the school can't afford even the cheapest computers. These students cannot possibly expect to compete with the children from that other world where schools get the best of modern-day laboratories, the newest of computer labs and computer banks in individual classrooms, and where teachers have enough time per student each day to work one-on-one with an eager learner. U.S. schools may be democratic, but they are not equal.

Education is the single most necessary asset one needs to move up in this society. Other factors are important, but education provides the ladder to climb up out of poverty. Poor people stay poor when they cannot get better jobs because they do not meet the requirements. They may be intellectually capable, but their lack of the academic or vocational training limits them. Yet present-day systems of taxation and school funding have made it impossible for poor towns and cities to provide their children with the tools they need to get ahead. Although the federal and state governments make contributions to local school systems, together their grants are likely to pay much less than half the yearly school budget. Poor towns cannot provide the same quality education that rich, suburban towns can because each city or town is primarily responsible for the cost of educating its young.

Consequently, poor schools produce children ill-prepared to compete. A Georgetown University study showed that students from the schools with the worst physical problems have the worst test scores. Schools rated "excellent" produce students whose scores are significantly higher. "I don't think a kid who is too hot or too cold or too hungry or too scared can really learn in a classroom. Kids know if something is important, because you take care of it," says Maureen Berner of the federal government's General Accounting Office.[6]

STABILITY OF SCHOOL

The conditions of our schools are not the only problem. Too often, children are forced to move from school to school. Five-year-old Mark and four-year-old Marlon are brothers. For now, they're painting with watercolors in a Chicago shelter school. This is their first day at the Playschool. Marlon looks ragged and dirty, and he seems only slightly aware of his surroundings. Mark explains that his house got "burnt up." When the teacher says "Pardon?" Mark explains that Marlon did it. "Yeah . . . I was in the bathroom . . . and then Marlon, he was screamin' and cryin'. . . . There be all this smoke an' stuff. I couldn't hardly even see. And my grandmama told me 'Get some water!' But we couldn't do it by ourself."

Mark and Marlon have just reached public-school age, but for them, a permanent place to live may be months and even years away. They are among the many children of welfare whose education will be jeopardized because of such crises as fire, eviction, or domestic violence. The Playschool is connected to a public shelter in which Mark's family will now live until the state finds them permanent housing. Its goal is to foster emotional development and reduce stress for these children. The teachers are skilled at helping them to express their fears. They do this by allowing plenty of free play, table games, and art, water, and sand play. The teachers know that acting out is to be expected from children trying to cope with their unsettled lives, and they do the best they can to help children learn acceptable social skills and express their ideas.

While model programs such as the Playschool can bring stability to children's lives, they will still experience far more problems because of the impermanence of their homes and the changing of schools. One of the most difficult tasks they face is fitting in. Being poor often exposes children to ridicule. Being *new* and poor makes ridicule almost a certainty. Children can be inordinately cruel to one another. They have not yet learned the need for tolerance, and they place great value on sameness. Thus a person who is different is guaranteed to have a hard time in school.

John Stower, from Orange County, California, is glad that for a while, he does not have to go to school. Before his family was evicted, he was picked on daily by the children in his second-grade class. "They don't like his shirt or they don't like his pants," his mother explains. "It's not high fashion enough." John agrees. "That's why I hate school," he says. "If there wasn't all those kids, I'd love [it]."[7]

Under these circumstances, children learn many defensive tactics to get by. Marcelino is seventeen. "At school I am talking and smiling all the time like it's no problem. You could go to any of my schools and ask any teacher, 'Does he get moody and does he withdraw from people?' and they'll say, 'No!'" But smiling and talking do not make Marcelino's pain go away. They lost their home when his mother had to flee her abusive boyfriend. Marcelino has learned that the safest way to defend himself is never to let anybody get too close. So he avoids other students. He even skipped his senior-class breakfast. "I don't think I would enjoy myself. I don't think I would fit in there. People talking and enjoying themselves—I don't think I would be able to relate to that," he says.[8]

Children who go to the same school year after year, even in the poorest areas, consistently do better than children who are bounced around from school to school. These children lose days, even weeks, of learning. The routine of being in school is disrupted, and the importance of school, under these circumstances, grows weaker. These children are more likely to repeat grades, miss out on needed services such as speech therapy or remedial reading or gifted education, and in the long run, these young people are the most likely to drop out of school.[9]

ABSENTEEISM

Not only are the schools most welfare children attend second-rate, and not only do welfare children face painful challenges to fitting in, but they will typically have greater difficulty learning and achieving in school. Falling asleep in class and failure to complete homework are two problems teachers consistently report. Absenteeism is another. For many youngsters, missing school is unavoidable—problems at home make it impossible for them to get to school. In Philadelphia, for example, one twelve-year-old boy missed many school days because he had to help his drug-addicted mother care for his little sister. Another, thirteen years old, had a mother dying of AIDS who could not care for herself. A fourteen-year-old girl who was beaten by a group of other girls missed three months of school. Another fifteen-year-old had a child and no one to help her care for the baby. According to John Woestendiek of the Philadelphia *Inquirer*, whole families of children miss school because they don't have bus fare or decent or clean clothes.

Others are afraid. Frankie Cruz, who manages an antitruancy program in Philadelphia, knows many of the reasons. "One kid spent an hour telling me the curriculum was not up to his standards. Finally, when I got him alone, he admitted he was being threatened by another student. He wouldn't say that in front of his parents. He was afraid his dad would think he was less of a man." Still others fear the embarrassment of being behind in their classes. "Sometimes I ask them to read," says Cruz, "and they barely can. And they know that when they get called on to read . . . everybody is going to laugh at them."[10]

Denise Stiglich says she started skipping school in the seventh grade because her friends did, but two years later, Denise was skipping months at a time because she feared the violence at Lincoln High School in Philadelphia. Now, even though she knows she must get an education, doing so is doubly hard because she is much older than her classmates. She is still in the ninth grade. "When you get so far behind, there's no sense in going back. I'm in class with a bunch of little girls, and it's uncomfortable to think they might know more than you. It's embarrassing when you don't know the answer and some little thirteen-year-old raises her hand and says, 'I know it.'"[11]

But not all students understand the need for education and the importance of being in school. At one high school, three carloads of students made monthly escapes to a local mall to shoplift. They often bagged more than $1,000 in merchandise, which they'd bring to someone's house for auction. "Bummin's jams" are the day-long parties students plan at empty houses or abandoned buildings. Those who go spend their school days drinking alcohol, smoking marijuana, and having sex.[12]

The statistics in Philadelphia reflect a trend nationwide in school systems that have no efficient way to track down students. Fewer than three of every four high-school students come to school each day. The average number of days missed by Philadelphia high-school students amounts to two months of every ten-month school year. More than half of all students' absences are unexcused. "It's like a drug," one truant says. "Once you start you can't stop—even though it's boring. Part of it is all your friends are cutting. But you know what I think a lot of it is? A lot of it is being lazy."[13]

When children are excessively truant, the only recourse school administrators have is to take the children and their parents to court. Truancy court can be an extremely frightening place because it is here that the state can exercise the right to fine parents for their children's absences and can remove children from their homes.

Judge Edward Summers was once a truant officer, so he is especially well equipped and knowledgeable when it comes to getting kids to school. He hears more than one hundred cases a day, so Summers has no time to listen to lengthy excuses from children or their parents. He is known for the tongue-lashings he gives when excuses don't add up. His treatment is effective for some parents, who leave the courthouse determined to make their children go to school. "This guy ain't messing around," Janice's mother told her. Janice had missed 166 days of middle school, so the judge had threatened the mother with jail. "I'm not going to jail. I'll tell you that right now. I'll be calling the school and checking. I'll take you there myself." Some children leave the courthouse sobbing, fearful that the judge is going to take them away from their families.

Unfortunately, others aren't intimidated by Judge Summers or the justice system. Gwendolyn Mason, a welfare mother of six children who each missed more than two months of school, leaves the courthouse seething. "Yes, I gave him a dirty look, and yes, I said a dirty word," she admits. "I just couldn't believe how he treated us, especially the lady who had been living in a shelter, and he was going to fine her and take her kids." Mason says her kids couldn't go to school because the family's gas was turned off due to a leaking gas line. The children couldn't take showers, and they had no clean clothes. "I wasn't going to send them to school all dirty and nasty . . . but the judge didn't want to hear nothing. . . . He's sitting up there in his high chair looking down his nose at us. . . . He should exchange places with some of the mothers he was incriminating—step out of his shoes into our shoes and come deal with it like we do," she says.[14]

Rather than rely on the justice system to get children to come to school, many systems institute original and creative approaches. One is an incentive program being tried in Ohio. Teen mothers who regularly go to school receive a bonus of $62 a month until they graduate; mothers who miss school or drop out find their welfare checks reduced $62 a month. This program has a proven record, but many criticize it as punitive. Others say that rewards can backfire if people begin expecting payment for everything they do. One teen mother who stayed in school and kept her attendance at an acceptable level, also said that for many she knows, getting an education is not the priority. "People I know are just after the extra money," she said.[15]

But not all feel this way. Stephanie McGinnis, age eighteen, is going into her third year of eleventh grade. "I came back this year because I want to have a future. I don't want to go to high school, but I want to go to college. Isn't that weird? I'm not leaving high school until I'm finished. If I'm a junior when I'm eighty, I'll still be going. I can see it now, my kids will be telling me, 'Mom, don't cut high school today.'"[16]

Another truant who vows he's going to start going to school every day says: "Kids that go to class everyday—I don't really understand why kids like that are considered nerds. They're gonna' be the ones with the nice cars and places to go. They're gonna' be the people that have some-thing. Those kids aren't nerds. They're strong. They're strong to be able to say, 'Screw that cutting party, I'm going to school.'"[17]

DROPPING OUT

"I hated school. It was overcrowded. Teachers didn't care. I never knew who my counselor was. After a while, I began spending my time sleeping in class or walking the halls. Finally I decided to hang out on the streets. That was it. End of school," says one New York City dropout.[18]

He's not alone. In the last several years in Boston, Mass-achusetts, more students were dropping out than graduat-ing. In Detroit, in rural Louisiana and Alabama, and in New York City, as many as 30 percent drop out of school before they graduate. Some racial groups are doing better than oth-ers. The most recent statistics (1995) indicate that both the black poverty rate and the black dropout rate are decreas-ing. Black students are doing better in both school and the workplace.

For those students of any race who leave school for uncertain futures, and the millions who graduate that are unable to read or write, however, the future looks very grim. They will face a lifelong struggle to remain off the welfare rolls. Most will not make it. The National Education Associ-ation believes that they will cost U.S. taxpayers $75 billion a year in lost tax revenues, crime, crime-prevention costs, unemployment, and welfare. Their burden to each person who pays taxes exceeds $800 a year.[19]

Programs designed to keep young people in school have had a sketchy success rate. Some experts believe the reason is that grant money is being spent on students beyond help-ing. "Taking children who are already at risk and who already have one foot out of the school is worth the effort, but it doesn't pay the kind of dividends that the long-term approach pays," says the head of one of the Bank Street College of Education's training institutes. The money has to be invested in programs that help children early. But long-term programs that begin in elementary school are the least likely to get funding because people are always looking for quick results, not results that won't show up for eight or more years. It is far more difficult to alter the habits and the outlook of students who are already adolescents, and that is the kind of student most dropout programs try to help.[20]

FAILURE TO LEARN

Unstable homes, improper nutrition, physical neglect, inequality of education, and illiteracy take a terrible toll on children. Their failure to learn, to go to school regularly, and to graduate is a direct result of a system that does not provide equal learning opportunities and environments to all students. Their frustration, unhappiness, and lack of hope is the only possible outcome. As we shall see in the next chapter, these children face additional obstacles that prevent them from achieving their potential. The streets and neighborhoods in which they are forced to live because of their poverty often seal their fates by drawing them into a world of gangs, guns, drugs, and death.

EIGHT

THE STREETS

Where poverty reigns, the buildings are pocked with holes from stray bullets. If one happens to look down at the sidewalk at the wrong time, human bloodshed may have stained the concrete. It is not unusual for children to pass buildings or entryways hung with the yellow tape that police use to protect a murder scene until it can be investigated. At night, the sounds of shooting are so common that many residents merely pause, waiting a panicked second or two for a bullet to career through a window or wall. Then life goes on as usual. Death where poverty reigns is always very much a part of life.

While not all welfare children are forced to live in impoverished neighborhoods, many are. Their families' circumstances and their lack of resources limit their choices. They have to live where rent is cheap or where the government subsidizes housing, which is usually in crime-ridden public projects. They find themselves crowded in among others just like themselves—poor people with few options. Some of them will miraculously grow up psychologically healthy enough to assume normal lives; some will even grow up stronger for the hardships they have endured.

THE SURVIVORS

For children growing up in Harlem, a borough of New York City, to walk to and from school, to stand on the street corner talking with friends, or to sit on the family stoop, even in broad daylight, is to invite danger. While Laverne Defense waits for her grandson Rasheed to come home from school one afternoon, she hears the sounds of gunfire and she thinks surely he must be dead. He always rounds the corner of 112th Street and Eighth Avenue at exactly the same time each day. She knows Rasheed is street smart, that he knows enough to watch for any car that mysteriously slows down as it approaches. But those things don't matter when drive-by shooters take aim at children not much more than four feet high. This time, the shots hit their targets. Three boys, ages fourteen to sixteen, lay bleeding. One dies. The police are not certain why they have been chosen for a hit.

Rasheed's grandmother can only feel relief—Rasheed has stayed late at school to try out for the track team. He will live to see another day. "This is Revelations we're living in," Mrs. Defense declares, referring to the biblical end of the world. "Believe me. The Bible spoke of this, the Koran—everyone spoke of this time, nearly two thousand years after Christ. The judgment. The chaos."[1]

Mrs. Defense is a deeply religious woman. Perhaps that is why her grandson Rasheed may have a chance. He was previously an intern at the prestigious firm Morgan Stanley, and Peter Henkel, a vice-president, now pays his $2,550-a-year tuition at Cardinal Hayes, the renowned Catholic boys' school. "This kid is special," Henkel told reporter Chris Smith. "Something inside Rasheed figured out a long time ago where he was going in life."[2]

Rasheed is a leader. He is vice-president of the student council and cocaptain of the school's bowling team. He plays after-school church basketball and organizes food drives for homeless people. The neighborhood kids "call me white boy," he laughs. But he doesn't let their jibes bother him at all. "It makes me feel good. They know I'm about school."[3]

Rasheed may appear too lucky to be a role model for other young people in his neighborhood, but only if they know nothing about him. His father is in prison. He writes Rasheed and encourages him to be proud of who he is. His mother hanged herself five years ago. Rasheed found her. "She had me when she was only sixteen, so we didn't have much of an age difference. We did anything and everything together." Yet these traumas have not crushed Rasheed. Though he knows pain, he also believes that people have to go on with their lives. "Say you're the CEO of a company, and your sister dies," he explains. "Awright, yes, she dies and that's terrible, that's tragic, but what are you going to do? Like stop working and become a bum? And your excuse is going to be your sister died? . . . A lot of things have come in my path. I could have given up. But I just can't."[4]

Rasheed's future looks bright. He has been accepted to Boston College, Providence, Syracuse, Lehigh, the University of Massachusetts, and Colgate. He has decided on Colgate because of the trees, because of the safety. He has his goals, his dreams. Somehow out of poverty, Rasheed has managed to find reason to hope. "What happens with a lot of kids is they only see the now," Rasheed says, looking around. "They don't see the future."[5]

THE VICTIMS

Shavon Dean, on the other hand, has no future. Nor does her murderer, Robert "Yummy" Sandifer. Shavon was fourteen on August 1994 when she walked her friend home at dinner-time for the last time. On the street, her path crossed that of Yummy's, an eleven-year-old Black Disciple gang member with a police rap sheet and a reputation pages long. Police think that Yummy had been assigned the shooting of someone in the neighborhood as revenge for an insult or a bad drug deal. But instead of a drive-by shooting, Yummy decided to do it face-to-face. "It was just an initiation ceremony, [so he could have done] it from a car. But to go right up to the victims, that means he was trying to collect some points and get some rank [in the gang] or maybe a nice little cash bonus," one gang expert explained.[6] Yummy strode out into the middle of a crowd of kids playing football, raised his 9 mm semiautomatic and opened fire. He hit others, but Shavon took a bullet to the head and died within minutes.

The crime was so bizarre, so astonishing, that all of Chicago was stunned. Soon the area was crawling with police and media reporters, everyone searching for Yummy. The pressure was so intense that his own gang members began to feel as if Yummy was a serious liability. Yummy must have realized that the gang wanted to get rid of him. He called his grandmother for help, but when she tried to meet him with some clothes, he didn't show. Later that night, shaking and scared, he begged a neighbor to call her for him so that he could turn himself in. Before she could do so, he once again disappeared. Gang members located him and either coaxed him or forced him down to a railroad underpass within gang territory. He was found lying dead in a mud puddle, with two bullets to the head.

"Nobody didn't like that boy. Nobody gonna miss him," said a thirteen-year-old. A local grocer from whose store Yummy had repeatedly stolen, said: "He was a crooked son of a b———. Always in trouble. He stood out there on the corner and strong-armed other kids. No one is sorry to see him gone."[7] At his funeral, the only picture the family had to put on his coffin was a police mug shot. The minister entreated the mourners to "Cry if you will, but make up your mind that you will never let your life end like this." Parents brought their children to the funeral hoping that maybe the sight of dead Yummy would scare them out of their own dangerous behaviors. What they saw was a boy so small that he was too short for some amusement park rides, a boy dressed in a loose tan suit, a child surrounded by stuffed animals. Everyone gaped at the stitches on his face where the bullets had exited.

While perhaps Yummy's death was fitting punishment for the death of Shavon Dean, one has to ask who should be punished for the life and death of Yummy Sandifer. Monsters are made, not born.

Some would say that Yummy Sandifer's life led inevitably to his and Shavon's untimely deaths. His mother, Lorina, was the third of ten children from four different fathers born to Janie Fields, whom psychiatric reports described as "a very controlling, domineering, castrating woman with a rather severe borderline personality disorder."[8] At fifteen, Lorina was pregnant. Yummy was the third of her eight children. Yummy's father, convicted on drug and weapons charges, did not stay long. Lorina claimed he was too hot-tempered. Having dropped out of high school in the tenth grade, she got her own apartment, became addicted to crack, and lived on AFDC.

In 1984, Yummy's brother was blinded because his mother did not follow through on his doctor's instructions. At twenty-two months, Yummy had to be taken to Jackson Park Hospital for bruises and scratches. Within a few months, his sister arrived at the same hospital with second-degree and third-degree burns on her genitals. The nurse did not believe the story Lorina told her about the girl's falling on the radiator, but it wasn't until a year later that the courts finally took action. The neighbors called police, reporting that Lorina's children were routinely being left alone. When the police removed Yummy and his brothers and sisters, he had long welts on his left leg and cigarette burns on his shoulder and buttocks. Still, his mother claims, "I never beat my kids. I gave him all the attention I could."

His mother, only twenty-nine, has a record of forty-one arrests, most of them for prostitution. She thinks the system is at fault, that something could have been done to prevent Yummy's death. "They could have saved him and rehabilitated him. When he started taking cars, they should have put him away then and given him therapy," she declares.[9]

Perhaps the system should take most of the blame. Instead of getting Yummy real help, their solution was to give his grandmother custody. Her neighbors in Roseland were not happy to have Janie Fields for a neighbor. Her house was more like a hotel, with some ten of her children and some thirty of her grandchildren coming to live and leaving with every passing day. "They are dirty and noisy, and they are ruining the neighborhood. . . . All those kids are little troublemakers," said one man who lives a few doors away. The neighbors signed a petition to force them out, all to no avail.

When Yummy came to live with his grandmother, he soon became the neighborhood bully and extortionist. He regularly scared other kids into giving him money. He was truant from school during the day, but broke into it at night. He stole money. He burned cars. If he wanted to, he cursed children and adults alike. People found that trying to do something about Yummy was a waste of time. If they spoke to his grandmother, she might yell at him, but he'd just go on doing whatever he pleased. If they called the police, the most authorities could do was to pick him up and bring him home. He was too young to lock up.

His youth, in fact, made him a prime target for gang recruiters, who prefer using children as drug runners and hit men because the law can't punish them as it can adults.

They are also eager to please and impress senior gang members. As one gang member explained it:

> He's this small little punk but wants a name, right? So you make him do the work. 'Hey, homey, get me a car. A red car. A red sports car. By tonight. I'm taking my woman out. Or hey, homey, go find me $50. Or hey, little homey, you wanna be big? Go pop that nigger that's messing with our business.[10]

Unfortunately, these children are not likely to last long in the world of gangs, drugs, and violence. "If you make it to nineteen around here, you are a senior citizen," explains Terrance Green, who happens to be nineteen.

By the time those in Yummy's world were through with him, he was probably beyond hope. According to one psychiatrist who evaluated Yummy before his final days, he was full of self-hate, lonely, illiterate, and wary. When the examiner asked him to complete the sentence "I am very . . ." his immediate response was "sick."

Still, a neighbor across the street from Yummy's house said the boy was not all bad. "He just wanted love. If he was alone, he was sweet as jelly." His twelve-year-old buddy Kenyata Jones added: "Everyone thinks he was a bad person, but he respected my mom, who's got cancer. We'd bake cookies and brownies and rent movies. . . . He was my friend, you know? I just cried and cried at school when I heard about what happened. And I'm gonna cry some more today, and I'm gonna cry some more tomorrow too."[11]

These young people, Rasheed from Harlem, Yummy from Chicago, represent the extremes of welfare children. One boy will likely rise above all those forces that would conspire to destroy him. The other lost his battle. He is a victim of a society that all too often ignores the needs of children.

People trapped in predatory neighborhoods rife with

poverty and neglect, neighborhoods like Rasheed's and Yummy's, are horrified by the violence and by the waste of young lives that they see daily. But for some, there is no escape. Thus the offspring of even the strongest families are jeopardized. "Alienated is too weak a word to describe these kids," says Edward Loughran, a ten-year veteran of the juvenile-justice system in Massachusetts. "They don't value their lives or anyone else's life. Their values system says, 'I am here alone. I don't care what society says.' A lot of these kids are dying young deaths and don't care because they don't feel there is any reason to aspire to anything else."[12] Or as Matt, a boy from San Francisco, put it:

> You know, I once took four hits of acid, double-soaked. That's like taking eight hits at once. Then I walked across a high bridge, figuring I wouldn't make it and that would be fine. . . . You learn to survive. But you also learn not to care if you don't.[13]

NINE

WELFARE'S SUCCESSES AND FAILURES

What was to be done about a welfare mother who had nine children by five different fathers? A woman who dropped out of high school and had a baby before she turned sixteen? Who waitressed for a while but then in 1982 went on welfare, where she remains, even today? A child of welfare herself, she points a blaming finger at her mother, who, she says, could easily have worked but chose to "stay on the dole" for thirty years.

When AFDC provided this woman with a decent three-bedroom townhouse with dining, den, and laundry rooms in a lovely nonwelfare neighborhood, she shoplifted and periodically ended up in jail. She was so threatening and abusive that within a two-year period, police had to be summoned to her home seventy-two times. She admits she "knocked [one neighbor] on her butt," but that the neighbor "had it in for me."[1] Finally, when her neighbors forced her out, the house was left filthy and damaged.

Perhaps her community thought such a woman was only worthy of scorn, and perhaps it was natural to want to cut her off from all support, but she had children. To punish her was to punish blameless victims. What else could the government do at this point, but help her find another place to live? This time she got an $87,000 townhouse, with four bedrooms and two-and-one-half baths. Her boyfriend of the moment told welfare he was living with his parents, but they spent most of the time together. They managed to get a king-sized waterbed, three color televisions, cable, and some state-of-the-art audio electronics, but soon the bedroom wall had a hole in it, the floors were littered with clothes and boxes, and she was complaining that welfare did not pay her enough to cover her electricity, water, and phone bills.[2]

And the children? Her first husband had to take custody of the oldest four. Her first child won't have anything to do with her. She doesn't know where the second is. She hasn't seen the third since he was two, and then it was only for about thirty minutes. The fourth was placed in foster care as an infant. Her fifth and sixth have each had two babies out of wedlock and are now living on welfare. The last of her children have been taken away and placed in foster care, but she vows she will get them back. Even though her welfare payments stop until she does get them back, she is not looking for a job. She suffers, she says, from "stress."

When writers Rachel Wildavsky and Daniel Levine traveled across the country to interview welfare recipients for their article "The True Faces of Welfare," they met Marie, and they chose to profile her because they felt she represents a type of welfare recipient that is all too common. Marie forces the government to make hard choices, choices that perhaps in another age and place would never have to be made. In another age, Marie would have had to change her ways, or she could not have survived. Certainly, her children could not have survived, not all nine of them. And they, like Marie herself, might never have lived to produce ever more children of welfare.

But the question remains—What is to be done about the children of welfare? How can a program have the desired effect of getting those dependent on welfare off the dole without systematically abusing children? Here is where the great difficulty lies.

A Difficult Problem

Part of the problem is that everyone forgets that welfare has only one purpose. According to Mary Jo Bane, a former social services commissioner for the State of New York, "The welfare system is in the business of writing checks and filling out forms. It's not in the business of getting people to work." AFDC was never meant to do more than "provide temporary assistance" to mothers and children. Yet it is being blamed for creating "generational dependency, taxpayer subsidy of illegitimacy, and failure to develop in recipients the discipline needed to end dependency."[3] Welfare and AFDC are only intended to provide a safety net. If people are to be prevented from needing such a net, then other programs must be designed to do the job.

Another part of the problem is that before HR3734 was signed into law, a record thirteen million Americans were getting AFDC. At present, one in seven children is on relief. Unemployment, a problem for economists and businessmen, is forcing more families to turn to welfare every day. And while welfare is being blamed for creating long-term dependency, lawmakers have been steadily increasing the numbers of people eligible for it by including poor, two-parent families and by creating education and training programs that tend to keep people on welfare for longer periods. Medicaid eligibility has also expanded, and some funding even provides day-care assistance.

A third part of the problem is the increasing cost of welfare programs. Economically, higher costs come at a very poor time. In the late 1980s and early 1990s, recession hit the nation very hard. People do not have the spending power they once had, and job security has all but disappeared. Yet taxpayers are being asked to spend more for intensive education and training for welfare recipients so that they can find better jobs with better futures.

While more families need welfare, while more families are eligible for welfare, and while greater sums are needed to help them, however, no one can point to convincing proof that all the effort and money is paying off. According to Manpower Demonstration Research Corporation's recent review of such welfare-to-work programs, even the most intensive, expensive, ambitious programs only reduced the welfare rolls by 8 percent.[4] Even more dismaying is that since 1965, the government has spent $5.4 trillion dollars (in constant 1993 dollars) and things are worse than ever.[5] In fact, the more the government has spent on welfare, the greater the problem has grown. For example, while welfare spending has increased 900 percent since the 1960s, illegitimacy also increased 400 percent.[6]

GETTING AT ITS ROOTS

Almost everyone thinks they know what is causing the problem, but few agree. Mario Cuomo, the former governor of New York, says "it's a lack of jobs. It's growing poverty. Its a low-wage economy."[7] Others point out that actually, employment rates among young whites and blacks with little education are better. Even if the country could reach full employment for everyone, they say, "it doesn't give disadvantaged kids more skills or create career paths, it doesn't necessarily pay them more than they can earn from a life of crime and drug dealing and it doesn't provoke young men to suddenly marry the mothers of their children."[8]

Some experts think our greatest problems stem from deadbeat dads who fail to take responsibility for their children, leaving the government to deal with the mess they've made of things. Others think that poor women are to blame, that if they would only lift themselves up by their bootstraps, they could work their way out of poverty. They blame women for laziness or lack of willpower.

Just as few experts can agree about the source of the welfare problem, few can agree about the direction the government should take to correct the problem. Three ideas seem to generate the greatest interest.

Workfare

President Clinton is a strong proponent of workfare. The goal of workfare is to get people working. To do so, the government would educate and train welfare recipients for up to two years. At the end of those two years, welfare payments would be cut off for all those able to work.

The plan has several strengths. Under it, welfare could never become a way of life. People would not expect the government to provide for them indefinitely. For those who want to work and to stand on their own, this program would provide the support they need. Recipients could attain a sense of personal dignity; taxpayers would be less resentful.

Unfortunately, the costs for programs that really do the job might be in the billions of dollars. Mothers would need not only job training, but also child care and health benefits until they could pay these expenses themselves. Even more elusive, however, is the answer to who will provide the jobs? There are not enough jobs for everyone. Consequently, the government would have to create jobs just to keep people working, and that would be more expensive, in the long run, than just ignoring the whole problem.

LEARNFARE

Because the key to obtaining jobs that pay enough to support families is education, many people believe that learnfare programs are the best approach to reforming welfare. Wisconsin, for example, punishes families if children miss too much school. The pressure is put on mothers (and fathers if they are present) and young people themselves to get up and go to class. The family can lose as much as $100 a month if they don't. That is a lot of money for a welfare family. Theoretically, the program gives children the incentive to stay in school and get their diplomas, a major step in becoming independent. But for more than half the state's families, attendance actually declined. Worse, rebellious teenagers suddenly had a new weapon to use against their parents. They could threaten to skip school if they did not get their way. The program does save the State of Wisconsin money. It cut the benefits of sixty-six hundred families because of their children's poor attendance, saving taxpayers $3 million.

KIDFARE

This reform is meant to stop women from having additional children while on welfare. Until recently, a newborn in the house entitled the family to an additional $64 a month from AFDC. But no more. Now a woman who has additional children will have to spread her monthly welfare check just that much thinner, which means less for everyone. This plan should eliminate the incentive to have children just to get extra money. In the long run, that can slow the growth of the welfare rolls. It also forces welfare mothers to do the same kind of responsible decision making that middle-class women have always had to do. Middle-class women who cannot afford children usually do not have them until they can.

The problem, of course, is that if all welfare mothers were capable of responsibile decision making, they might not be on welfare in the first place. Forcing them to subsist on less money per child victimizes children, but it probably does little to make their mothers more responsible.

Programs That Work

Oregon is trying a new "Jobs Plus" program that locates employers willing to hire a welfare recipient who has no employment experience. Jobs Plus workers are paid the state minimum wage by the company, but the company is then reimbursed by welfare. The recipient still receives Medicaid, housing assistance, and child-care allowances, but wages become the main source of income rather than a welfare check. Kentucky is trying the same thing. For Susan Ison, who was six years on AFDC, it is the beginning of a new life for her and her seven-year-old daughter. She has been hired to work in accounting at a Kentucky electrical supply company. "I'm trying to earn my way there. I'm trying awful hard. I'm prouder. I feel better about myself," she says.[9]

Katherine Mims grew up in Harlem with her mother, four brothers, one cousin, and a fourteen-year-old pregnant aunt. Because everyone in her apartment was a welfare recipient, Katherine stood a good chance of becoming a teenage mother herself. She even dropped out of school in the ninth grade. But then she heard about the Family Life and Sex Education Program of the Children's Aid Society, an agency dedicated to helping inner-city boys and girls get a life of their own before creating a new one. Rather than preach against sex, this program tries to provide structure and opportunities for achievement in the lives of teenagers. The incentive at the end of the program is a free undergraduate education at Hunter College in New York.

Through Children's Aid, Katherine got private tutoring so that she could finish school. She took lessons in swimming and tennis, career counseling, and got a summer job. Now she is working on a degree program at Hunter. She has married, but has no intention of having children until she finishes. She knows she has come a long way from that twelve-year-old who first entered the Children's Aid program. "I didn't think I'd make it out of high school," she admits.[10]

Some incentive programs spend money to keep people healthy, like the Prudential Health Care Plan that pays pregnant Medicaid patients in Baltimore $10 to keep their appointments. Poor expectant mothers often do not have time to tend to their health; health care is often their lowest priority. But good prenatal counseling is not only essential to the health of the baby, but also cost effective. Early discovery of problems can often prevent serious and very costly problems later, after the child has been born.

Other programs offer family support and counseling. Of the two hundred women who have attended Washington, D.C., General's maternal health project, not one has abandoned her child. Angela Holland knows how great an accomplishment that is. At age seventeen, Holland had the first of her three daughters. The four of them lived in an abandoned house, without gas or heat, while her abuse of crack drew her farther and farther into the world of drugs. Eventually, she abandoned her babies. "That's when I started thinking about killing myself," she told reporter David Van Biema. But instead she turned to D.C. General. There she attended group meetings, worked with dietitians and social workers, discussed problems with recovering addicts, and took parenting classes. "I learned how to feed my children—how to fix a healthy meal and not feed them hot dogs and beans all the time. I learned you don't have to spank them; you can just talk to them."

Today Angela has kicked her habit, gotten married, given birth to a drug-free fourth daughter, and regained custody of the other three girls. "Sometimes I want to pull my hair out," she says, "but I wouldn't change nothing. I've never felt this kind of love before. I have a life ahead of me and four beautiful girls who depend on me."[11]

Annie Williams's daughter Natale is an honor-roll student in the eleventh grade. She is planning a career in medicine. Annie and Natale lived on welfare for a number of years before she found out about the Black Women's Wellness Center in Atlanta, Georgia. There she got help finding educational programs for herself and child care for Natale. "Most women think, 'What's the use even trying?'" she says. "Until I got in with this empowerment group, I didn't even know you could do such a thing." Today Annie has a job that pays $20,000 a year at the Wellness Center, and her daughter looks forward to her own future.[12]

Sean's wardrobe was comprised of shoplifted clothes. No wall or idling subway car was safe from his spray paint. He still has a scab over his left eye, but it is from a fight he didn't start. Today Sean works as a messenger for a photo lab, and he does his paintings on a privately sponsored mural project on 107th Street. He credits the Amsterdam Avenue youth program's DOME Project for the changes in his behavior and outlook. Sean spent two years in DOME's intensive junior high; later, he was selected for a ten-week trip to a kibbutz in Israel. He learned a great deal from both, including how important the people who loved him were. "A lot of times I can't even believe I made it this far," Sean says. "It feels like it could all still disappear."[13]

MAKING A DIFFERENCE

These successful programs seem to share several characteristics. First and foremost, they are amply funded. Few good programs are forced to show bottom-line, immediate results. They tend to have long-term goals and future expectations as opposed to quick fixes that are superficial or temporary. Their grants are not constantly in danger of being cut, so the program can concentrate on getting results rather than preserving funding. Those delivering the services have small enough caseloads to provide adequate attention to the people they are helping. Facilities are located where they are needed and where people can find and get to them.

Because most successful programs have long-term goals, they tend to be carefully planned and structured. Postprogram monitoring and evaluation are part of their systematic follow-through and assessment. They are in a state of constant modification, based on the assessment of their effectiveness. They have clearly defined goals and a dedicated staff.

The successful programs are as varied as the people they attract. Across the nation, public and private funding have made creative programs available to those on welfare. When welfare does not work, human beings are lost, if not to death, then to loneliness, isolation, and degradation. When welfare programs work, they change the lives of people who might otherwise become chronically welfare dependent, both a burden and a loss to their society.

OF FROGS AND
FUTURES

In her book *Tyranny of Kindness*, author Theresa Funiciello tells the shocking story of a seven-year-old girl whose mother chose to send her and her four siblings back to Allah, her Muslim God, rather than have them face a life of poverty and peril without a father. According to all reports, Fatima Ali was a loving, concerned, and responsible mother. She kept her apartment and her children clean and neat, and the family was never any trouble to its neighbors. Unfortunately, having recently been separated from her husband, Mrs. Ali did not have enough money to pay the rent. For Islamic women, especially women with children, to be without a husband is to be nearly worthless. To be without any means of support, however, was to stand on the edge of an abyss. For Mrs. Ali and her children, the descent into poverty, homelessness, the streets, welfare, welfare hotels, drugs, prostitution, violence, and degradation seemed all but inevitable.

On an October day in 1989, Mrs. Ali decided that she and her children had but one hope, and that was to be delivered unto Allah. She had her children remove their clothes. Later, she explained that "We came into this world with nothing, and that's how we [were] going to leave."[1] And then she began praying. Calmly, in a state of deep religious affirmation, Mrs. Ali lifted her daughter out of the window. A fire truck just returning from a call saw the small girl dangling from her mother's arms, ten stories up. They tried desperately to turn around in time, but just as the firefighters arrived, the child hit ground. Immediately, two firemen began resuscitation procedures, while others raced into the building for the elevator. "We tried to stabilize her," said one. "Just as she was breathing on her own, I heard people screaming. I couldn't imagine what the commotion was, because it looked as though she was going to make it. I looked up and saw another small child spinning down." Mrs. Ali had dropped a second child out the window. He fell directly on top of his sister. "After that we couldn't get a pulse from her, and blood was spilling from her mouth."[2]

As Mrs. Ali was about to lift her one-year-old to the window, firemen burst through her door and grabbed her. She urged her remaining children to go quickly out the window, but frightened, they did not comply. Mrs. Ali believed she had failed herself and her family. She believed that what she had done was the only proper and responsible thing she could do. She might have abandoned her children, but a devout Islamic could never do that. She might have headed for the nearest welfare office. But she knew what that meant and felt she could not, in good conscience, do that either. In her mind, returning to Allah was their only salvation.

The State of New York, however, considered it murder. She was arrested, and her children were placed in foster care. While it may be difficult for people who do not share Mrs. Ali's religious convictions to understand how a mother could drop her children to their deaths, the fact remains that Mrs. Ali wholeheartedly believed she had to do what she did. She had been a responsible married lady who had delivered five children believing that her husband would support them. She had no reason to believe that she and her babies would be left without means of support.

THE INEQUITIES OF THE WELFARE SYSTEM

In fact, had Mr. Ali died instead of leaving the family, Mrs. Ali would have had far different prospects. First of all, instead of being viewed as a "left wife" and a failure, she would be a guiltless widow. Instead of being treated as a welfare deadbeat, she would have been supported and helped by state and local agencies. Instead of begging for meager welfare support from the state, she would have been "entitled" to generous social security "survivor" benefits. The difference between her welfare allotments and the survivor benefits would have been an extra $1,000 per month, enough for her family to stay in their apartment, in their safe neighborhood. Mrs. Ali would even be entitled to stay home and raise her children, at least until they were grown. But if she did get a job at any time, her social-security check would still arrive every month and the amount of the benefit would remain unaltered, no matter how much money Mrs. Ali could make on her own.

The well-known children's story "The Frog Prince" seems especially appropriate when the real life of Mrs. Ali, the abandoned wife, and the projected life of Mrs. Ali, the widow, are compared. In the story, a wicked witch casts a spell upon a handsome prince, turning him into an ugly frog. Unless the prince could find some lovely young girl willing to kiss him, he was compelled to remain forever slimy and green. Fortunately for the prince, he did find a lovely maiden, and not so willingly, she did kiss him. That story ends happily ever after.

In real life, all too many stories end in tragedy. Mrs. Ali

might not have been cursed by a wicked witch, but because of the way our welfare system works, she turned into a frog when her husband left her. She was isolated, she was without resources, and the only social safety net afforded her made her as much of a social outcast as any frog.

Mrs. Ali's need to transport herself and her children beyond this life evidences just how terrifying it is to find welfare one's only alternative. Much of the way that the welfare system is administered and many welfare policies seem designed to humiliate recipients. "We are not garbage!" one young man shouted at a California welfare officer after countless attempts to get his family's allotment corrected. First the office misplaced his birth certificate. Then when a check finally was issued a month later, he received a mysterious second check for $102. Frightened that welfare might consider his holding onto it welfare fraud, he reported the mistake. Even though the state's computer had made the error, he was told to immediately return the check to the welfare office, some thirty miles away. He stood in line, was sent to another line, then waited in another office even longer. When he made the mistake of sitting momentarily on the security guard's desk, he was ordered to stand. "I'm sick of your goddamn system!" he shouted, having lost the last shred of patience he had. "You're treating us like garbage!"[3]

The consequences for young people are even worse. When Robert Coles traveled the country talking to children who had fallen into the welfare safety net, he often had them draw their families and their homes to gain insight into how they felt about their lives. An eleven-year-old girl who lived in a welfare motel refused to draw the dilapidated building in which she was forced to live. "It's not anyone's home; it's where you stay if you don't have a home," she said. Moments later, she added that actually the motel was a kind of home. "Rats live there," she explained.[4] Social worker Jenny Nelson of Portland, Oregon, found that young children often are so ashamed of their condition and so fearful that they are responsible for their families' problems, they do not want to look at themselves in the mirror.[5]

These children are the products of a society that thinks welfare is too kind, too generous, and too easily obtained. They are the very people who will suffer the most if the welfare reforms just enacted are administered without additional programs to help recipients retrain and acquire jobs. "If compassion were not enough to encourage our attention to the plight of our children, self-interest should be," former Governor Mario Cuomo declared a few years ago.

Self-interest should be a strong argument for making every possible attempt to better the lives of the children of welfare. They are growing up unprepared to compete for jobs. Their options are limited. They are growing up in neighborhoods rife with crime and violence, in environments devoid of hope. They lack self-esteem. They lack a sense of belonging. And many of these children are growing up angry because the society that should be embracing them has instead "relentlessly ignored their needs."[6] "The inattention to children by our society," warns Marian Wright Edelman, the founder of the Children's Defense Fund, "poses a greater threat to our safety, harmony, and productivity than any external enemy."[7]

The welfare reforms being passed today are reforms aimed at adults. It is adult dependency that the new two-year limits are designed to end. It is adult irresponsibility that has led lawmakers to abolish the additional money welfare grants for each new child. Although on paper these may seem strong incentives to find work and to avoid additional pregnancies, they can jeopardize the health, security, and safety of children unable to do anything about their situations. "Get them off the dole, two years and out?" asks Carol Bevan of the National Council for Adoption. "What does that mean if you're a two-year-old?"[8]

Many feel that the first thing that this nation must do is to clarify for itself the reasons why Americans feel they must help those who need it. From a purely selfish point of view, flourishing societies and hordes of people dying in the streets for lack of food, shelter, and health care cannot co-exist. Few people can step over bodies on their way to work or to school without demanding that something be done.

In addition, armies of those without food, shelter, or hope are dangerous armies, for they have little to lose. Among hungry people, survival takes precedence over morality. Unless we intend to sacrifice the freedom of move-ment we so cherish and instead live in protected fortresses much like the aristocracy did in the Middle Ages, preventing the formation of such armies is in our own best interests.

There are other reasons, of course, that are less self-serving. We know from history and experience that provid-ing people with the tools to succeed can awaken in them a great capacity for productivity and good. Civilized societies provide every "reasonable opportunity" for those in need to get on their feet. They strive to increase the number of jobs, so that everyone who wants to work can work. They pro-vide job training, so that those willing to learn have the opportunity to obtain decent jobs for decent pay. They pro-vide solutions to some of the obvious problems, such as transportation, food, clothing, health care, shelter, and how to care for small children. Their aim is to build self-worth and confidence in those who lack it. In monetary terms, such programs are costly—even more costly than ignoring the problem and allowing the cycle to continue.

Providing every "reasonable" opportunity implies a limit to how much and to how long a person should be entitled to aid, and that aid is a temporary measure. When a crisis occurs, when a job is lost because a company must lay-off its workers, when a woman is widowed or divorced and left without means to support her family, when illness strikes the head of the household, most people believe that citizens should be entitled to extensive but temporary aid. A laid-off worker might have to retrain for some other job, a widowed or divorced mother might need counseling, job training, and child-care services to get and hold a job, and the spouse of an ill head-of-household may have to prepare to become the primary wage earner. There should be no loss of honor for people who find themselves in trouble, as long as they are willing to work to pull themselves out.

Although chronic welfare families are but a small portion of those in need of welfare, their cost to the public is disproportionately high. Almost everyone agrees that these people need to work for their own living, even if the government has to subsidize their pay. Most can learn how to be independent. In doing so, they can also provide a working role model for their own children, instilling in them a sense of personal responsibility.

In communities comprised of proven achievers who hold high expectations for their children, the teenage birthrate is dramatically lower than in poor communities where young people have little hope of doing any better than their needy parents. These impoverished surroundings become "a breeding ground for the kind of risky, dysfunctional behavior . . . that most high-achieving teenagers would view as foolishly imperiling their gilded futures," writes journalist Michael Leahy.[9]

If there are no prospects for the future, adolescents have little reason to guard against pregnancy. Similarly, if society can offer young people no reason to hope for better things, and therefore no motivation to work for them, then it is not surprising that many will choose to depend on the system for their meager needs.

These children are our nation's greatest resource.

Among them, if we do nothing, the artists, the scientists, the writers, the astronauts, and the political leaders of tomorrow can remain, like frog princes, forever cursed by poverty and despair. In the next few years, state and local governments will be taking over the responsibility for their social welfare. With this new power comes an awesome responsibility to see that the mistakes of the past will not be repeated in the future.

SOURCE NOTES

ONE: THE FACES OF POVERTY

1. Ron Fitten, "Poor Children: Life Collides With Dreams," Seattle *Times/Post-Intelligencer*, June 16, 1991.
2. Marilyn Gardner, "Poverty's Legacy—Fragile Families, Vulnerable Babies," *Christian Science Monitor*, December 18, 1989.
3. Ibid.
4. Ibid.
5. Ibid.
6. David Van Biema, "Mother and Child Reunion," *Time*, January 21, 1994.
7. Chris Smith, "Generation Next," *New York Magazine*, May 23, 1994.
8. Ibid.
9. Ibid.
10. "Childhood Lost," Hartford, CT *Courant*, January 19, 1992.
11. Michele Ingrassia and John McCormick, "Why Leave Children With Bad Parents?" *Newsweek*, April 25, 1994.
12. Michael Leahy, "Seeking Respect, Finding Trouble," Little Rock *Democrat-Gazette*, March 20, 1994.
13. Ibid.
14. Karen Peart, "Life on Welfare," *Scholastic*, March 11, 1994.

15. Rachel Wildavsky and Daniel Levine, "The True Face of Welfare," *Reader's Digest*, March, 1995.

16. Ibid.

17. Ibid.

18. Ibid.

19. Ibid.

20. Leahy, "Seeking Respect, Finding Trouble."

21. Smith, "Generation Next."

TWO: "THE WELFARE"

1. Marvin Olasky, "History's Solutions," *National Review*, February 7, 1994.

2. Ibid.

3. Ibid.

4. Ibid.

5. Myles Gordon, "The Fight for Welfare Rights," *Scholastic*, March 11, 1994.

6. Herbert Buchsbaum, "The Welfare Debate," *Scholastic Update*, March 11, 1994.

7. Mike McNamee, "Pain for the Poor: A Play for the Middle Class." *Business Week*, April 13, 1992.

8. John DeMott, "Welfare Reform Could Work," *Nation's Business*, August 1994.

9. Jon D. Hull, "The State of the Union," *Time*, March 7, 1995.

10. Tom Morganthau, "The Entitlement Trap," *Newsweek*, December 13, 1993.

11. DeMott, "Welfare Reform Could Work."

12. Pete Axthelm, "Somebody Else's Kids," *Newsweek*, April 25, 1988.

13. Charles Murray, "Keeping Priorities Straight on Welfare Reform," *Society*, July–August, 1996.

14. William Bennett, "What to Do About Welfare," *Commentary*, March 1995.

15. Brenda Wilson, "Dealing with the Underclass," *Editorial Research Reports*, November 1989.

16. DeMott, "Welfare Reform Could Work."

17. McNamee, "Pain for the Poor: A Play for the Middle Class."

18. Holly Sklar, "The Upperclass and Mothers N the Hood," *7 Magazine*, March 1993.
19. Peart, "Life on Welfare," *Scholastic*, March 11, 1994.
20. Ibid.
21. Ibid.
22. Ibid.
23. Ibid.
24. Ibid.
25. Gretchen Webster, "Area Welfare Recipients Applaud New Regulation," Norwalk, CT *Hour*, October 1, 1994.

THREE: NO ONE TO TURN TO

1. Holly Sklar, "The Upperclass and Mothers N the Hood," *7 Magazine*, March 1993.
2. Phil Sudo, "The Underclass," *Scholastic*, March 11, 1994.
3. Guy Gugliotta, "The Persistence of Poverty," Washington *Post*, National Weekly Edition, January 3–9, 1994.
4. Ibid.
5. Jonathan Freedman, *From Cradle to Grave* (New York: Atheneum, 1993).
6. Ibid.
7. John Dilulio, "What to Do About Welfare," *Commentary*, December 1994.
8. Brenda Wilson, "Dealing With the Underclass," *Editorial Research Reports*, November 1989.
9. Richard Lacayo, "Unraveling the Safety Net," *Time*, January 6, 1994.
10. John McCormick, "America's Third World," *Newsweek*, August 8, 1988.
11. William H. Freivogel and Martha Shirk, "Child Support: Who Pays? Out-of-Wedlock Births: A Caseload from Hell," St. Louis *Post Dispatch*, May 3, 1993.
12. Sheryl James, "His Own Worst Enemy," Detroit *Free Press*, October 3, 1993.
13. Ron Fitten, "Poor Children: Life Collides With Dreams," Seattle *Times/Post-Intelligencer*, June 16, 1991.
14. Karen Peart, "Life on Welfare," *Scholastic*, March 11, 1994.

15. John DeMott, "Welfare Reform Could Work," *Nation's Business*, August 1994.
16. Beth Lovern, "Confessions of a Welfare Mom," *Utne Reader*, July–August, 1994.
17. David Whitman, "The End of Welfare as We Know It?" *U.S. News and World Report*, June 3, 1996.
18. Sklar, "The Upperclass and Mothers N the Hood."
19. David Whitman, "The Key to Welfare Reform," *Atlantic Monthly*, 1987.
20. Lacayo, "Unraveling the Safety Net."
21. Nancy Gibbs, "The Vicous Cycle," *Time*, June 17, 1994.

FOUR: FAMILY TIES

1. Michael Leahy, "Seeking Respect, Finding Trouble," Little Rock *Democrat-Gazette*, March 20, 1994.
2. Ibid.
3. Ibid.
4. Chris Smith, "Generation Next," *New York Magazine*, May 23, 1994.
5. William Tucker, "All in the Family," *National Review*, March 6, 1995.
6. Ibid.
7. Walter Williams, "The Welfare Debate," *Society*, July–August, 1996.
8. Leahy, "Seeking Respect, Finding Trouble."
9. William Bennett, "What to Do About Welfare," *Commentary*, March 1995.
10. David Popenoe, "Family Caps," *Society*, July–August 1996.
11. Ibid.
12. Charles Murray, "Keeping Priorities Straight on Welfare Reform," *Society*, July–August 1996.
13. Joanne Jacobs, "Children Who Are Having Children," San Jose *Mercury News*, April 7, 1993.
14. Ibid.
15. Beth Lovern, "Confessions of a Welfare Mom," *Utne Reader*, July–August 1994.
16. Tucker, "All in the Family."
17. Ibid.

18. Nancy Gibbs, "The Vicious Cycle," *Time*, June 17, 1994.

19. Ibid.

20. Ibid.

21. Ibid.

22. Heather MacDonald, "The Ideology of Family Preservation," *Public Interest* (Spring 1994).

23. Michele Ingrassia and John McCormick, "Why Leave Children With Bad Parents?" *Newsweek*, April 24, 1994.

24. Ibid.

25. Ibid.

26. Ibid.

27. Mary-Lou Weisman, "When Parents Are Not in the Best Interest of the Child," *The Atlantic Monthly*, July 1994.

28. Tom Morganthau, "The Orphanage," *Newsweek*, December 12, 1994.

29. Bennett, "What to Do About Welfare."

FIVE: HOME, SWEET HOME

1. Joanne Jacobs, "Children Who Are Having Children," San Jose, California *Mercury News*, April 7, 1993.

2. Ibid.

3. "The Children of the Homeless," *U.S. News and World Report*, August 3, 1987.

4. Frank Trippett, "Down and Out in L.A.," *U.S. News and World Report*, August 3, 1987.

5. Frank Gibney, "In Texas, a Grim New Appalachia," *Newsweek*, June 8, 1987.

6. Ibid.

7. Joseph Berger, "When School Offers Refuge to Homeless," *New York Times*, April 9, 1990.

8. Judith Berck, *No Place to Be* (New York: Houghton Mifflin, 1992).

9. Ibid.

10. Suzanne Daley, "Family Shelters: Crowds, Dirt, and Drugs," *New York Times*, May 8, 1989.

11. Jonathan Kozol, *Rachel and Her Children* (New York: Crown Publishers, 1988).

12. Berck, *No Place to Be*.

13. Ibid.

14. Brad Kessler, "Down and Out in Suburbia," *The Nation*, September 25, 1989.

15. Ibid.

16. Reginald Johnson, "State Funds 'Temporary' Motel Housing," Westport, CT *Fairpress*, March 1, 1990.

17. Laura Guerin, "Living on Welfare," Norwalk, CT *Hour*, August 19, 1995.

18. Sharon Cohen, "Hopes Fade in Troubled Cities: U.S. Poverty Getting Deeper," The Hackensack, New Jersey *Record*, June 26, 1994.

19. Robert Coles, "Lost Youth." *Vogue* July 1989.

20. Ibid.

SIX: FAILURE TO THRIVE

1. Laura Shapiro, "How Hungry Is America?" *Newsweek*, March 14, 1994.

2. Ibid.

3. Ibid.

4. Gary Drevitch, "The Safety Net," *Scholastic*, March 11, 1994.

5. Shapiro, "How Hungry Is America."

6. Ibid.

7. Ibid.

8. Ibid.

9. Ibid.

10. Jonathan Kozol, *Rachel and Her Children* (New York: Crown Publishers, 1988).

11. Guy Gugliotta, "The Persistence of Poverty," Washington *Post*, National Weekly Edition, January 3–9, 1994.

12. Marilyn Gardner, "Poverty's Legacy—Fragile Families, Vulnerable Babies," *Christian Science Monitor*, December, 18, 1989.

13. Kozol, *Rachel and Her Children*.

14. Gardner, "Poverty's Legacy."

15. John McCormick, "America's Third World," *Newsweek*, August 8, 1988.

16. Gugliotta, "The Persistence of Poverty."

SEVEN: UNEQUAL EDUCATION

1. Jonathan Kozol, "The New Untouchables," *Newsweek*, special issue, 1990.
2. Ibid.
3. Mary-Lou Weisman, "When Parents Are Not in the Best Interest of the Child," *The Atlantic Monthly*, July, 1994.
4. Ibid.
5. Ibid.
6. Ibid.
7. Melissa Weiner, "Homeless Children Struggle With Their Own Class Structure," Santa Ana *Orange County Register*, July 2, 1989.
8. Ibid.
9. Joseph Berger, "When School Offers Refuge to Homeless," *New York Times*, April 9, 1990.
10. John Woestendiek, "Truancy Rampant in the City," Philadelphia *Inquirer*, December 5, 1993.
11. Ibid.
12. Ibid.
13. Ibid.
14. Ibid.
15. Christine Gorman, "Dollars for Deeds," *Time*, May 16, 1994.
16. Woestendiek, "Truancy Rampant in the City."
17. Ibid.
18. Ibid.
19. Kozol, "The New Untouchables."
20. Berger, "When School Offers Refuge to Homeless."

EIGHT: THE STREETS

1. Chris Smith, "Generation Next," *New York Magazine*, May 23, 1994.
2. Ibid.
3. Ibid.
4. Ibid.
5. Ibid.

6. Nancy Gibbs, "Murder in Miniature," *Time*, September 16, 1994.

7. Ibid.

8. Ibid.

9. Ibid.

10. Ibid.

11. Ibid.

12. Nancy Gibbs, "Shameful Bequest to the Next Generation," *Time*, October 8, 1990.

13. Pete Axthelm, "Somebody Else's Kids," *Newsweek*, April 25,1988.

NINE: WELFARE'S SUCCESSES AND FAILURES

1. Rachel Wildavsky and Daniel Levine, "The True Faces of Welfare," *Reader's Digest*, March ,1995.

2. Ibid.

3. John DeMott, "Welfare Reform Could Work," *Nation's Business*, August, 1994.

4. "Why the Welfare Mess Gets Messier," *U.S. News and World Report*, November 25, 1991.

5. David Popenoe, "Family Caps," *Society*, July/August, 1996.

6. Ibid.

7. "War on Welfare Dependency," *U.S. News and World Report*, April 20, 1992.

8. Ibid.

9. DeMott, "Welfare Reform Could Work."

10. Richard Lacayo, "Want a Baby? First Get a Life," *Time*, June 20, 1994.

11. David Van Biema, "Mother and Child Reunion," *Time*, January 21, 1994.

12. Emily MacFarquhar, "The War Against Women," *U.S. News and World Report*, March 28, 1994.

13. Chris Smith, "Generation Next," *New York Magazine*, May 23, 1994.

TEN: OF FROGS AND FUTURES

1. Theresa Funiciello, *Tyranny of Kindness*, (New York: Atlantic Monthly Press, 1993), 40.

2. Ibid., p. 3.

3. Anne Fadiman, "A Week in the Life of a Homeless Family," *Life*, December 1987.

4. Robert Coles, "Lost Youth," *Vogue*, July 1989.

5. "The Children of the Homeless," *U.S. News and World Report*, August 3, 1987.

6. Nancy Gibbs, "Shameful Bequest to the Next Generation," *Time*, October 8, 1990.

7. Ibid.

8. Tom Morganthau, "The Orphanage," *Newsweek*, December 12, 1994.

9. Michael Leahy, "Seeking Respect, Finding Trouble," Little Rock, *Democrat-Gazette*, March 20, 1994.

FURTHER READING

BOOKS

Berck, Judith. *No Place to Be*. New York: Houghton Mifflin, 1992.

Blankenhorn, David. *Fatherless America: Confronting Our Most Urgent Social Problem*. New York: Basic Books, 1995.

Brown, Robin, ed. *Children In Crisis*. New York: H. W. Wilson Company, 1994.

Fontana, Vincent, M.D. *Save the Family, Save the Child*. New York: Dutton, 1991.

Freedman, Jonathan. *From Cradle to Grave*. New York: Atheneum, 1993.

Kozol, Jonathan. "The New Untouchables." *Newsweek*, special issue, 1990.

Liebow, Elliot. *Tell Them Who I Am*. New York: Macmillan, 1993.

Sander, Joelle. *Before Their Time*. New York: Harcourt, Brace, Jovanovich, 1991.

Switzer, Ellen. *Anyplace but Here*. New York: Atheneum, 1992.

PERIODICALS

Becker, Gary S. "Revamp Welfare to Put Children First." *Business Week*, March 30, 1992.

Bennett, William J. "What to Do About the Children." *Commentary*, March 1995.

Berger, Joseph. "When School Offers Refuge to Homeless." *New York Times*, April 9, 1990.

Berger, Joseph. "Dropout Plans Not Working, Study Finds." *New York Times*, May 16, 1990.

Berstein, Aaron. "The Case of the Climbing Welfare Rolls." *Business Week*, May 13, 1991.

Buchsbaum, Herbert. "The Welfare Debate." *Scholastic Update*, March 11, 1994.

Carlson, Allan. "Divorce and Illegitimacy." *Society*, July–August 1996.

Conniff, Ruth. "Welfare, Ground Zero: Michigan Tries to End It All," *The Nation*, May 27, 1996.

DeMott, John S. "Welfare Reform Could Work." *Nation's Business*, August 1994.

Dornbusch, Sanford M., Melissa Herman, and I-Chun Lin. "Single Parenthood," *Society*, July–August, 1996.

Drevitch, Gary. "The Safety Net." *Scholastic*, March 11, 1994.

"Education in Decay." *U.S. News and World Report*, September 12, 1994.

Fadiman, Anne. "A Week in the Life of a Homeless Family." *Life*, December 1987.

Funiciello, Theresa. *Tyranny of Kindness*. New York: Atlantic Monthly Press, 1993.

Gates, David. "History of the Orphanage." *Newsweek*, December 12, 1994.

Gergen, David. "Reforming Welfare at the Very Top." *U.S. News and World Report*, April 20, 1992.

Gibbs, Nancy R. "Murder in Miniature." *Time*, September 16, 1994.

———. "Millions of American Families Hold Two or Three Jobs." *Time*, June 26, 1995.

———. "The Vicious Cycle." *Time*, June 17, 1994.

"Give This Workfare Plan a Chance," editorial. *Business Week*, May 20, 1996.

Glenn, Norval D."Welfare Experimentation." *Society*, July–August, 1996.

Gordon, Myles. "The Fight for Welfare Rights." *Scholastic*, March 11, 1994.

Gorman, Christine. "Dollars for Deeds." *Time*, May 16, 1994.

Guerin, Laura. "Living on Welfare." Norwalk, CT. *Hour*. August 19, 1995.

Herbert, Bob. "Scapegoat Time." *New York Times*, November 16, 1994.

Hull, Jon D. "The State of the Union." *Time*, March 7, 1995.

Ingrassia, Michele, and John McCormick. "Why Leave Children With Bad Parents?" *Newsweek*, April 25, 1994.

Klein, Joe. "The Out-of-Wedlock Question." *Newsweek*, December 13, 1993.

Koretz, Gene. "It's Getting Harder to Put Young America to Work." *Business Week*, March 30, 1992.

Kozol, Jonathan. *Rachel and Her Children*. New York: Crown Publishers, 1988.

Kronenwetter, Michael. *Welfare State America: Safety Net or Social Contract?* New York: Franklin Watts, 1993.

Lacayo, Richard. "Unraveling the Safety Net." *Time*, January 6, 1994.

———. "Want a Baby? First Get a Life." *Time*.

LeVert, Marianne. *The Welfare System: Help or Hindrance to the Poor?* Coon: Millbrook, 1995.

Lovern, Beth. "Confessions of a Welfare Mom." *Utne Reader*, July–August 1994.

MacFarquhar, Emily. "The War Against Women." *U.S. News and World Report*, March 28, 1994.

McCormick, John. "America's Third World." *Newsweek*, August 8, 1988.

McNamee, Mike. "Pain for the Poor, a Play for the Middle Class." *Business Week*, April 13, 1992.

Morganthau, Tom. "The Entitlement Trap." *Newsweek*, December 13, 1993.

———. "The Orphanage." *Newsweek*, December 12, 1994.

Murray, Charles. "Keeping Priorities Straight on Welfare Reform." *Society*, July–August, 1996.

Nathan, Richard P. "Is It Necessary to Be Brutal?" *Society*, July–
August, 1996.

Offner, Paul. "How Deadbeat Dads Can Reform Welfare." *Time*,
August 1, 1994.

Offner, Paul. "A Better Solution to the Welfare Mess. Welfare Dads."
Time, February 13, 1995.

Olasky, Marvin. "History's Solutions." *National Review*, February 7,
1994.

Peart, Karen N. "Life on Welfare." *Scholastic*, March 11, 1994.

Rom, Mark. "Reversing America's Welfare Magnets." *USA Today*,
March 1992.

Shapiro, Laura. "How Hungry Is America?" *Newsweek*, March 14,
1994.

Silverstein, Ken. "Give Me Shelter." *Scholastic*, March 11, 1994.

Sudo, Phil. "The Underclass." *Scholastic*, March 11, 1994.

Tucker, William. "All in the Family." *National Review*, March 6, 1995.

Van Biema, David. "Mother-and-Child Reunion." *Time*, January 21,
1994.

Wackerman, Daniel T. "Mind's Eye," *America*, January 13, 1996.

Walsh, Catherine. "Perspectives." *America*, November 11, 1995.

"War on Welfare Dependency." *U.S. News and World Report*, April 20,
1992.

Weisberg, Jacob. "How Low Can You Go?" *New York Magazine*, January 15, 1996.

Weisman, Mary-Lou. "When Parents Are Not in the Best Interest of the
Child." *The Atlantic Monthly*, July, 1994.

Whitman, David. "The End of Welfare as We Know It?" *U.S. News &
World Report*, June 3, 1996.

Whitman, David, and Dorian Friedman. "His Unconvincing Welfare
Promises." *U.S. News and World Report*, April 20, 1992.

———. "Michigan's Phony Welfare Numbers." *U.S. News and World
Report*, February 6, 1995.

Wildavsky, Rachel, and Daniel Levine. "The True Face of Welfare."
Reader's Digest, March, 1995.

INDEX

abortion, 6, 44, 47, 48

absenteeism, 81–84, 100

acquired immunodeficiency syndrome (AIDS), 8, 53, 81

Adoption Assistance and Child Welfare Act of 1980, 55

adoption, 6, 47, 53, 57

Aid to Families with Dependent Children (AFDC), 9, 11, 19, 21–23, 40, 43, 46, 49, 60, 66, 91, 95, 97, 100, 101

alcohol abuse, 10, 33, 34, 82

Ali, Fatima, 105–108

Appalachia, 19, 33, 61, 73

Barrett, Rose, 48, 49

battered women, 38, 66, 80

Black Women's Wellness Center, 103

boarder babies, 7

Boys Town of Omaha, Nebraska, 57

Brace, Charles, 16, 17

Bray, Rosemary, 28

child abuse, 8, 17, 34, 38, 52–56, 91, 92

child care, 12, 13, 24, 38, 52, 54, 57, 81, 97, 99, 101, 103

Children's Defense Fund, 109

civil rights movement, 28

Clemans, Gina, 5, 15

Clinton, Bill, 21, 22, 25, 42, 99

Coles, Robert, 68, 108

college education, 5, 18, 29, 35, 59, 84, 89, 101, 102

colonias, 61

crime, 52, 85, 87, 90–92, 95, 98, 103, 106, 109

dead-beat dads, 37, 51, 52, 99

Dean, Shavon, 89–91

Defense, Laverne, 88

DOME project, 103

drugs, 6–11, 14, 33–36, 40, 48, 50, 52, 53, 55, 58, 65, 66, 70, 73, 81, 82, 86, 90–94, 98, 102, 103, 105

Edelman, Marian Wright, 109
education, 18, 20, 23, 24, 39, 43, 44, 58, 77–79, 82, 84, 89, 97–100, 103
Efrid, Gwen, 44
Emergency Assistance Unit (EAU), 63–65
emergency medical care, 39, 74
failure to thrive, 69, 72
family preservation, 54–56
Family Support Act of 1988, 49
Family: Past and Present, The, 45
Fields, Tamisha, 44, 45
food relief programs, 70, 71, 73
food stamps, 11, 19, 21, 23, 32, 33, 39, 46, 49, 50, 60, 70–72
foster care, 7, 8, 49, 52–57, 96, 106
Funiciello, Theresa, 105
gangs, 34, 86, 90, 92, 93
Gardner, Marilyn, 72
George, Erica, 10, 46
ghettos, 33–35
government-subsidized housing, 5, 6, 15, 43, 46, 47, 60, 67, 68, 72, 79, 87, 95, 96
Great Depression, 17, 18
group homes, 57
health care, 11, 13, 20, 21, 49, 58, 73–75, 99, 102, 110
Henkel, Peter, 88
high-school dropouts, 10–12, 14, 25, 27, 30, 33, 50, 81, 84–86, 91, 95, 101
Holland, Angela, 102, 103
homelessness, 6, 18, 52, 60, 89, 105, 110
HR3734, 22, 23, 28, 42, 97
human immunodeficiency virus (HIV), 7

illegitimate children, 11, 22, 24–26, 36, 37, 43, 45, 46, 96, 98
immigrants, 19, 20, 39, 45
Income Maintenance (welfare) Center, 62, 63
Ison, Susan, 101
job skills and training, 6, 18, 19, 23, 24, 39, 78, 97–99, 109–111
Jobs Plus, 101
Johnson, Lyndon B., 19, 32, 33
Kellom, Marquita, 43, 45
Kozol, Jonathan, 62, 73
Lamm, Richard, 20
learnfare, 100
Levine, Daniel, 96
Livingston, Tangela, 14
"Lost Youth," 68
low-income housing, 66–67
Malinowski, Bronislaw, 45
malnutrition, 69–72, 75, 86
Mason, Gwendolyn, 83, 84
McGinnis, Stephanie, 84
Medicaid, 11, 21, 22, 24, 32, 39, 46, 74, 97, 101, 102
middle class, 18, 75, 100
Mims, Katherine, 101, 102
Mitaynes, Sean, 7, 8
Morris, Leslie, 10
Mothers' Assistance program, 16
Murray, Charles, 24–26, 48
Muskus, Christopher, 8, 9
National Council for Adoption, 109
National Education Association, 85
New Deal, 18
New York Children's Aid Society, 17, 101, 102
New York City, 16, 28, 29, 64, 65, 77, 85, 88

orphan trains, 17
orphanages, 16, 52, 56, 57
parental neglect and abandonment, 7–9, 17, 34–37, 52, 55, 70, 86, 91, 92, 94, 102, 106
Popenoe, David, 48
poverty, 5, 6, 26, 27, 32, 33, 39–41, 48, 70, 74, 78–81, 86, 87, 89, 94, 98, 99, 105, 112
"Poverty's Legacy—Fragile Families, Vulnerable Babies," 72
prenatal care, 6, 73, 102
Proposition 187, 20
prostitution, 16, 92, 105
public shelters, 6, 38, 60, 62–65, 72, 79, 84
Rachel and Her Children, 62
racial statistics, 5, 24, 31, 40, 41, 46, 47, 85
residential treatment centers, 57
Rivera, Eulalia, 40, 41
Rothenberg Elementary School, 76, 77
Sandifer, Robert "Yummy," 89–94
school meal programs, 21, 70
schools, 35, 76–82
Section 8, 66, 67
single parenthood, 8, 10–15, 22–25, 35, 37, 39, 46–49, 52, 105, 107
Social Security, 18, 107
social workers, 10, 29, 48, 53, 56, 108
soup kitchens, 60, 70, 72
Summers, Edward, 83
taxes, 16, 19, 22, 23, 27, 41, 58, 78, 85, 98, 99
teenage pregnancy, 7, 10–14, 25, 27, 34, 35, 40, 41, 43–49, 51, 52, 58–60, 73, 81, 84, 89, 91, 95, 101, 102, 111

Temporary Assistance for Needy Families (TANF), 22
Torrey, Patricia, 77
truancy, 82–84, 92
"True Faces of Welfare, The," 96
Tucker, William, 45
Tyranny of Kindness, 105
unemployment, 18, 19, 41, 60, 72, 85, 97, 110
unemployment insurance, 18, 19, 21
urban campgrounds, 60–62
violence, 33–35, 52, 67, 79, 82, 86–88, 90, 92–94, 103, 105, 109
war on poverty, 19, 28, 32, 33
welfare:
abusers, 19, 39, 40, 41, 51, 71, 96, 100
Asian recipients of, 40
black recipients of, 24, 25, 35, 40
critics, 23–25
dependency, 13, 14, 23, 42, 50, 51, 97, 104, 109, 111
Hispanic recipients of, 40
hotels and motels, 60, 63, 65, 66, 72, 105, 108
reforms, 14, 20, 21, 26–28, 37, 50, 66, 109
resentment and shame, 28–30, 108, 109
subcultures, 51
white recipients of, 25, 40
Wildavsky, Rachel, 96
Wilson, Pete, 20
workfare, 99
working poor, 35, 59, 61, 67, 68, 75